THREE PLAYS

David Cregan

THREE PLAYS

WHISPERS ALONG THE PATIO
NICE DOROTHY
THE LAST THRASH

OBERON BOOKS
LONDON

WWW.OBERONBOOKS.COM

First published in this collection in 2001 by Oberon Books Ltd.
(incorporating Absolute Classics)
Tel: +44 (0) 20 7607 3637 / Fax: +44 (0) 20 7607 3629
e-mail: info@oberonbooks.com
www.oberonbooks.com

A catalogue record for this book is available from the British
Library.

PB ISBN: 9781840022452
E ISBN: 9781786821973

Cover illustration: Andrzej Klimowski
Cover typography: Jeff Willis

Contents

INTRODUCTION

Sam Walters

David Cregan is a unique playwright. To read a page of his dialogue is to enter a very specific world unlike that of any other writer I know. Those who learn to relish his very particular style almost always become enthusiasts. We rush around gaining converts, and if this publication of his latest plays were to be followed by re-publication of his earlier work, readers, and one would hope audiences, would be in for a treat.

Although, of course, he has had a distinguished and award-winning career as a radio dramatist, Cregan's plays are entirely theatrical. He understands the way theatre works. Every line is an action. No doubt a legacy of his early days at the Royal Court, where he was a member of a writers' group that took part in acting exercises, and even today, armed with knowledge learned with George Devine and Keith Johnstone, he might, somewhere, at some time, take a mask class!

Not for him the drabness of everyday naturalism. For while his plays are rooted in real life, there is a rhythm and a music in the writing. Cregan writes with style and wit. There is also speed and economy. No slow revelation of character, but rather an immediate declaration of intent.

> HARRIET: This is my Aunt Dorothy – oh, Billy.
> BILLIE: I'm sorry. (*Continues crying.*)
> DOROTHY: Shall I go?
> HARRIET: No, no. She'll dry out soon.
> DOROTHY: (*Over the sobs.*) I've been visiting my old mother which is quite a – are you sure she's going to stop?
> BILLIE: I'm mad because I love somebody who doesn't love me.
> DOROTHY: Oh dear.
> HARRIET: But we cured her with madrigals, so she's just pretending. She's my new flat mate.
> JUDY: I'm Judy, I'm promiscuous, and I don't cry.
>
> (*Nice Dorothy*, 1993)

The characters, and therefore the actors, turn on a sixpence. A word is said, a thought expressed, and the play changes direction, only to do so again seconds later.

> TANIA: (*Looking round.*) There's nowhere else unoccupied, I think.
> TONY: Do sit with me, it'll be all right. (*He smiles and then consults papers.*)
> TANIA: You mean I'll be safe?
> TONY: Yes, of course. And you won't be in my way.
> TANIA: I wasn't thinking of that.
> TONY: I was reassuring you.
> TANIA: Are you a policeman?
> TONY: Good heavens no. Is this your first visit to England?
> TANIA: Yes.
> TONY: Do you like it?
> TANIA: Why d'you want to know?
> TONY: Well, it's a nice country, isn't it. As nice as Austria?
> TANIA: I doubt it.
> TONY: Most people would say 'yes' to that question.
> TANIA: Why?
> TONY: To be polite. It eases relations to be polite.
> TANIA: You tell lies in England to make people like you?
>
> (*Whispers Along the Patio,* 2001)

His plays require the nimblest of performers and an attentive and agile audience. As performer and as audience you have to get on the wavelength of Cregan's writing. But once you are there, as it were, it really is a unique world full of great rewards and huge delight.

But the often farcical humour and extraordinary economy belie a real political and social involvement. His plays may appear to skim the surface. But the seeming inconsequentiality is highly deceptive. His characters are always striving to make sense of life and struggling in a morass of moral anguish.

> I'd like to know one thing only, and it's not a mysterious thing. Why is life difficult? There's no reason I know of why life should be difficult but everybody I've ever heard of has found it so. Of course, the difficulties are relative. I'm not Prince Hamlet, for example.
>
> (*Transcending,* 1996)

His latest play, *Whispers Along the Patio*, seems to me to be about a most important subject. The threat to any group, community, country even, when individuals allow their personal desires and wants to take precedence. But the idea is there beneath the surface, underpinning the play, as the farcical manoeuvrings of the characters spin the story along from moment to moment. For while there is pain and passion and eruptions of anger and hurt, there is also an enormous sense of fun. And it is that sense of fun allied to a love of what human beings can do with language that makes Cregan's plays uniquely joyful. But make no mistake, Cregan's purposes are serious. *The Last Thrash*, for example, may be funny, but the author's opposition to the private education depicted in the play is total.

I first came across David Cregan's plays in 1966 when, at the Traverse Theatre, Edinburgh, I was asked to be in a late night production of his play *The Dancers*. When I first read the play it completely mystified me. I gave it to my wife, Auriol Smith, who read it and returned it to me with the words, 'This is very funny.' 'Really?' I said. And my relationship with Cregan's plays began.

Like others before him, David Cregan made a false start as a novelist. But in 1965 he was taken under the wing of the Royal Court and it was there that his first plays were produced. *Miniatures* received a full-length Sunday Night without decor production. (Would that that idea could be revived, but now everyone is after 'production values'; I have even heard of play readings where there has been a lighting designer!) This was followed by his two short plays, *The Dancers* and *Transcending*. Then came his first main stage play, *Three Men for Colverton*. Later there was *The Houses by the Green*. Then, in 1969, his *Comedy of the Changing Years* opened the Theatre Upstairs.

But theatre directors move on, and those who had championed Cregan at the Court went elsewhere. Philip Hedley produced some Cregan when he was at the Midland Arts Centre, and David Cregan/Brian Protheroe pantomimes are still regularly seen at Stratford East. Caroline Smith directed *Poor Tom* at the Contact Theatre,

Manchester, and *Cast Off* at the Sheffield Crucible. And Rhys McConnochie directed *The Land of Palms* at Dartington. But from the 1970s onwards Cregan's theatrical home has been the Orange Tree Theatre in Richmond where, I think, fourteen of his plays have been produced, including six premieres, three of which are in this volume – *Whispers* as a co-production with the Stephen Joseph Theatre, Scarborough, where it began its run.

David Cregan commands great loyalty from those who have learned to trust and to enter his world. It is not that the overall subject matter of his plays would alarm (although it *might*), but rather that the expression of his concerns and the sheer theatricality of his invention leads some to exclaim, 'Am I supposed to be taking this seriously?' I have, on occasion, found myself having that initial reaction. The seeming flippancy has provided an easy excuse for those who are not prepared to delve beneath the surface. The answer is to delve, to discover the truth and reality of the situations and the characters, and then to come up to the surface again and allow the play to carry you along on waves of delight. All I can say is that, for me, discovering the plays of David Cregan, directing them and even, occasionally, acting in them, have been among the highlights of my theatrical life.

Sam Walters
Orange Tree Theatre, 2001

WHISPERS ALONG THE PATIO

Characters

MATHEW
a retired man of comfortable means

JUNE
his busy niece, about forty

TANIA
a foreign visitor, early twenties

TONY
a young salesman, mid twenties

HAROLD
a bus driver, late twenties

This play is written for the scenery to be changed in full view
where indicated, and as the dialogue is spoken.

Whispers Along The Patio was first performed by The Orange Tree Theatre Company at The Stephen Joseph Theatre, Scarborough, on 2 August 2001, with the following cast:

MATTHEW, Frank Moorey

JUNE, Jane Arden

TANIA, Cate Debenham-Taylor

TONY, Steven Elder

HAROLD, Jason Baughan

Director, Sam Walters

Designer, Pip Leckenby

Lighting Designer, Kath Geraghty

Costume Designer, Christine Wall

Stage Manager, Cath Booth

Deputy Stage Manager, Anne Baxter

Assistant Stage Manager, Emily Thurlby

ACT ONE

Scene 1

A patio, and at one side of the stage, a piece of lawn where a half-standard rose bush stands. MATHEW, a retired man of about sixty-five, is eating his breakfast in his socks and reading a newspaper. There is a walking-stick at the other end of the table and shoes beside him. After a moment he turns to the audience.

MATHEW: (*To the audience.*) It's marvellous here. It's utterly beautiful, inside and outside. I am completely untroubled, and the sun is shining on my breakfast and what more could there be in the world than to drink coffee and read the *Guardian* on a patio in Richmond? I always used to say to my wife, 'When one of us dies, I will go and live in Richmond.' My wife is a lovely person who went off eventually with a Hungarian lawyer, which is sad – I do admit that, one has to – but as she pointed out, she always thought that when one of us died she would go and live beside the Danube, so we may as well each have our dreams fulfilled while there was still, as it were, time. Or life, really. So the chance came, and there she is in Hungary, and here I am in Surrey, and she's quite right. I love it here – roses, little lawn, patio – and she loves it somewhere near the Danube Bend, I think it is, close to a place where Saga Tours call, so she often sees her friends, and they eat a lot of goulash together. Which is nice.

JUNE: (*Off.*) Hello? Uncle Mathew?

MATHEW: Ah. Hello.

JUNE: (*Off.*) On the patio as usual?

MATHEW: Yes.

JUNE: (*Entering.*) Not catching cold?

MATHEW: No.

JUNE: (*Placing package on table.*) Those who look after themselves (*With MATHEW.*) are the least trouble to others.

MATHEW: So your grandmother used to say.

JUNE: And isn't it a lovely day, though there's still a bit of dew on the grass. (*She moves to examine grass and the rose bush.*)

MATHEW: Is it Budapest or Bucharest where they eat goulash?

JUNE: Both probably, but I don't care for it.

MATHEW: I don't care for it either, but Hetty loved it, and I suppose her Hungarian lawyer does, too, in Budapest or Bucharest, and I just wondered which.

JUNE: Never mind which, Uncle, she's happy, so let go and move on, as they say.

MATHEW: Those who don't have to. I only mentioned her by accident. What's this?

JUNE: Some lunch I thought you' d like. Taramasalata.

MATHEW: Oh. Are you staying long?

JUNE: I want you to realise Aunt Hetty is very happy, and you can be happy, too, if you try.

MATHEW: I am happy. So it's nice to see you, thank you for lunch, and are you staying long.

JUNE: You just have to make the effort.

MATHEW: For what?

JUNE: To be happy.

MATHEW: I'm perfectly happy without doing anything but sitting on my patio, drinking coffee, and going to Art Galleries.

JUNE: Good. (*She exits to the kitchen side of the stage.*)

MATHEW: Hetty has been gone fifteen years, and I've never looked back, and nor has she.

JUNE: (*Off.*) Good.

MATHEW: She's even learnt Hungarian.

JUNE: (*Off.*) Good.

MATHEW: It's a silly sort of language only understood by Finns. June?

JUNE: (*Off.*) Don't the Hungarians understand it?

MATHEW: Of course they do. It's their language.

JUNE: (*Entering.*) You get confused a bit these days, don't you. (*She has secateurs.*)

MATHEW: No.

JUNE: I've got some news for you.

MATHEW: There's more coffee in the kitchen, so have a cup on the way out. What are you going to do?

JUNE: You drink too much coffee, you know. Gives you the dithers.

MATHEW: Don't touch that bush.

JUNE: I'm serious, Uncle. Too much coffee and you'll get the dithers. And you mustn't keep harping on about Aunt Hetty and the Hungarian.

MATHEW: Come away from that bush, tell me your news and go and get some more coffee.

JUNE: I don't want any.

MATHEW: I do.

JUNE: It's bad for you.

MATHEW: (*Great irritation.*) I like it! I shall drink it! And I do not have and never have had any symptoms of any illness from it, let alone the one you irritatingly call the dithers. Stop that! (*He goes towards the rose bush which JUNE is savaging.*)

JUNE: It's running wild.

MATHEW: It's free and happy!

JUNE: D'you use that walking stick?

MATHEW: You're taking all the buds.

JUNE: Have you had your pills?

MATHEW: There are no pills to have.

JUNE: I thought you were getting some for high blood pressure.

MATHEW: I don't have high blood pressure, so I don't have –

JUNE: If you go on drinking coffee –

MATHEW: Leave this bush and go.

JUNE: Right. It's all right. I'll get you some coffee, poisonous stuff. And I'll have that walking stick for the shop if you don't want it. (*She exits to the kitchen with what she has cut.*)

MATHEW: 1-2-3-4-5-6-7-8-9-10. I hate and detest taramasalata!

JUNE: (*Off.*) You love it, but go on, just get it off your chest.

MATHEW: I loathe it.

JUNE: (*Off.*) That's right.

MATHEW: Don't make me feel guilty. You're a kind woman, as we all know – (*To audience.*) she is, mercilessly kind, works for Help The Aged, and she –

JUNE: (*Entering with a pot of coffee.*) Talking to yourself?

MATHEW: Possibly. Now have some coffee and go.

JUNE: Put your shoes on, or your socks'll get soaked.

MATHEW: They are already.

JUNE: Those who take care of themselves –

MATHEW: I'm wriggling my toes in the dew and it's gorgeous.

JUNE: What you need, Uncle, is company. Company?

MATHEW: D'you know what company is?

JUNE: Pardon?

MATHEW: It's very rare, and is made up of people who are life-giving and wonderful, and who don't – it doesn't matter.

JUNE: Go on, Uncle, don't be afraid.

MATHEW: I'm not afraid. I'm polite.

JUNE: That's what I told them this morning.

MATHEW: Company is – Told who?

JUNE: Now then. Some very nice people.

MATHEW: I sense, June, we are reaching a moment that can't any longer be delayed. In future, I want you to leave me completely alone.

JUNE: I've got you a job.

MATHEW: There are times when even charming, polite, peaceful people want to put an axe through the heads of their relations.

JUNE: Why?

MATHEW: I don't want a job. I have a nice, middle class occupational pension that I sweated for years to get. I don't need to work. I don't want to work. I want you to go away and leave me, happy as I was, except I shall now walk through the dew in socks and feel sensual.

JUNE: Now that's not the whole truth, is it.

MATHEW: Yes, it is. I haven't felt sensual for years, so I've lots to catch up on. Keep away. (*Defensive of roses.*)

JUNE: You're always saying you feel past it, and how you'd like to have those skills again that enabled you to make such a valuable contribution to society.

MATHEW: I would never say anything so stupid.

JUNE: But you know it's true, and if you stay here doing nothing all the time you'll go funny.

MATHEW: I'll grow calm and quietly ecstatic, being a fortunate man whose only problem is an interfering niece buzzing round him like a hornet, destroying his garden. Furthermore, I do not want to make a valuable contribution to society, because I've done everything I can in that direction, and so far as I can see it hasn't worked. Oh – why do we ever wear anything on our feet? Oh! Oh!

JUNE: I think you're being very selfish.

MATHEW: Yes.

JUNE: Many men your age are making a very great contribution to society, and I would've thought –

MATHEW: I don't like society! It's mean and petty and preoccupied with mobile telephones.

JUNE: There's nothing wrong with mobile –

MATHEW: And supermarkets!

JUNE: There's nothing wrong with –

MATHEW: I do not want a job! And where've you put the buds?

JUNE: In the dustbin.

MATHEW: Not in water?

JUNE: I think you're very ungrateful, especially as the job I got you is helping with reading in schools.

MATHEW: Among the infant drug addicts and sex maniacs?

JUNE: Don't get silly. Just think how everybody loves you, and how children would thrive in your care. There's your coffee. And I'll have the walking stick for the shop. (*Takes it.*)

MATHEW: If I fall, you'll be blamed. (*Smiles.*) What did you mean, I need company?

JUNE: A job, I told you. People to talk to.

MATHEW: You didn't mean company like – just company.

JUNE: Of colleagues, yes.

MATHEW: Not company like – interlocking knees?

JUNE: No.

MATHEW: Did you know that more sexually transmitted diseases are passed on by the over sixties than any other age group?

JUNE: Put your shoes on.

MATHEW: No. You'll inherit if I die.

JUNE: Well, your taramasalata won't keep, so eat it up. I don't like leaving you like this. I'll go because I have to, but I may be back. Take care, Uncle. Uncle?

MATHEW: Have a nice day.

JUNE: Perhaps. (*She exits.*)

MATHEW: (*To the audience.*) Wet socks. Need I say more?
Ten minutes ago I just wanted to read the *Guardian* and go
tut about life. But company – the word rings out like bells
across fields. I mean, fifteen years – dear Hetty. I think I'll
visit Kew Gardens and meet Nannies with prams, young
students interested in burgeoning plants and hopefully long
lived oaks.
(*The scene is beginning to be removed.*)
It's dew between the toes that sets you on. One doesn't
have to die yet, not with wet feet murmuring wickedness.
(*Leaves the stage.*)

Scene 2

*The scene being set is a table and three chairs in an open-air cafe
in Kew Gardens. Enter TONY, a young salesman with a briefcase
who is speaking into a mobile phone. He also has a cup of coffee,
and the trace of a Yorkshire accent.*

TONY: Nige? Trouble is, Nige, there doesn't seem to be much
call for rat poison in Richmond. They're afraid it'll get to
their pets. Moggies and dachshunds by the look of it, alsa-
tions for the rugger players. Anyway, they prefer a deterrent, send the rodents round to the patio next door. Well,
I'm going to have a cup of coffee in Kew Gardens while
I think a bit. Yes, right, slaughter the squirrels. Become a
local issue. It's full of birds, actually. (*Laughs at what is being said to this.*) No, real ones. Well, perhaps, but I've a lot
of paper work. Speak to you soon, bye. (*He puts the phone
away, and goes to the table, arriving at the same time as TANIA,
a pretty young girl, well-dressed, with a very slight foreign accent
who also carries a cup of coffee and a plate with a cake on it.
They both put their cups down.*)
TANIA: I'm sorry.
TONY: Sorry?
TANIA: Wasn't I first?
TONY: No, but we can share.
TANIA: No, it's yours. (*Retrieves her cup.*)
TONY: Right. (*He sits and opens case and takes out papers or
personal organiser.*)

TANIA: (*Looking round.*) There's nowhere else unoccupied,
  I think.

TONY: Do sit with me, it'll be all right. (*He smiles and then
  consults papers.*)

TANIA: You mean I'll be safe?

TONY: Yes, of course. And you won't be in my way.

TANIA: I wasn't thinking of that.

TONY: I was reassuring you.

TANIA: Are you a policeman?

TONY: Good heavens no. Is this your first visit to England?

TANIA: Yes.

TONY: Do you like it?

TANIA: Why d'you want to know?

TONY: Well, it's a nice country, isn't it. As nice as Austria?

TANIA: I doubt it.

TONY: Most people would say 'yes' to that question.

TANIA: Why?

TONY: To be polite. It eases relations to be polite.

TANIA: You tell lies in England to make people like you?

TONY: It's not lying to be polite.

TANIA: In Europe we're very direct.

TONY: Good.

TANIA: You don't believe me?

TONY: We've only just met. Why should I lie?

TANIA: You thought I should say England was as nice as
  Austria even if I didn't think it was, when we had met even
  less time than when I said we Europeans are direct.

TONY: I didn't think you should. I said I thought you might.

TANIA: Have you ever been to Austria?

TONY: No.

TANIA: Nor have I.

TONY: I thought you sounded as if you came from Austria.

TANIA: I'm Macedonian. (*Glancing towards his papers.*) I
  should've thought you knew. Or could tell by my accent.

TONY: Can you tell where I come from by my accent?

TANIA: Leeds. There's a table over there, now. It's been
  interesting to meet you. (*She stands.*)

TONY: How did you know I came from Leeds?

TANIA: We have some soldiers in Macedonia, and they talk like you. By 'eck, chip oil, dead baring.

TONY: I don't talk like that.

TANIA: Not now, certainly, but once upon a time.
Good morning.

TONY: You're a bit of a surprise, aren't you. I can't tell whether you're daft or just rude. What are you doing here?

TANIA: I'm moving to that table over there, and I know what daft means.

TONY: You know the soldiers quite well, then

TANIA: They were on our side.

TONY: Which side?

TANIA: It's very complex, as perhaps you know. Good morning.

TONY: You haven't eaten your cake.

TANIA: It's stale.

TONY: If you haven't eaten it, how do you –

TANIA: (*Grabbing the cake from the plate she has left on the table.*)
You are too persistent!

TONY: I'm simply straightforward.

TANIA: No, I'm straightforward, you're a liar.

TONY: My name's Tony.

TANIA: My name's Tania, and I want to go to another table.

TONY: That one's gone.

TANIA: Then that one.

TONY: That's gone, too.

TANIA: You are a policeman, aren't you.

TONY: No.

TANIA: You don't frighten me.

TONY: You scare me.
(*She sits down again.*)

TANIA: Go on making your notes.

TONY: What are you doing in England?

TANIA: My papers are in order.

TONY: I mean what is it you do while –

TANIA: You're famous for this, aren't you. Keep the foreigners out, so the first thing policemen say to someone they meet in a cafe that sells stale cakes is 'What right have you to be here?'

TONY: I'm not a policeman.

TANIA: I have every right to be here. This is Kew Gardens
and I'm nicely dressed.

TONY: All right.

TANIA: So don't lie to me.

TONY: I haven't lied to –

TANIA: You told me you lied all the time.

TONY: I didn't.

TANIA: I'm going… (*She rises.*)

TONY: Right.

TANIA: You want me to go back to Macedonia? You think
I'm here to live off your social security? You're a fascist.

TONY: They do have those in Austria.

TANIA: Typical British stereotyping, turning all foreigners
into the Second World War.

TONY: Are you going?

TANIA: Why should I? (*She sits.*)

TONY: Either we're pleasant to one another, or you go and
frighten someone else.

TANIA: I didn't start this.

TONY: I didn't either.

TANIA: You said I should've lied to be polite. Yes, you did.
If you're so straightforward you should speak directly what
you think. Just try that. Go on. Be direct. Policeman or not.

TONY: You're bloody peculiar. If you weren't, I'd quite like
to know more about you. No, I'm not a policeman. I mean
I'd like to know you personally. Especially, if I'm honest –

TANIA: Yes?

TONY: I'd like to know what it's like to make love to you.
Peculiar and demanding, I expect.

TANIA: You won't find that out, certainly.

TONY: I'm not really sure that I want to, but you asked me to
be direct.

TANIA: I am not peculiar. Am I? The English soldiers in
Macedonia were very straightforward, so one simply said
'Bugger off' to them.

TONY: Are you going to say that to me?

TANIA: You are typically Western and arrogant, and I've
had experience of it before. The soldiers boasted they had
wives and girlfriends all over the Balkans, shedding babies
like feathers. They were proud of it.

TONY: Perhaps I should get on with some work.

TANIA: We Macedonians aren't Romanians, you know, we're spirited and independent. We aren't Bosnians, leaping into bed with every passing man, or Croatians, terrified of any kind of relationship, or Greeks wanting to own us, or Serbs or Albanians, shooting men and women the minute they get a chance –

TONY: You sound supersensitive and small minded.

TANIA: (*Rebuffed, stands, but is unable to leave.*) All this space in Kew Gardens and they haven't enough tables to sit at without being insulted.

TONY: Quite. (*Picking up mobile phone.*) If you don't mind, I have to speak to someone on business.

TANIA: What business?

TONY: I sell rat poison.

TANIA: There are rats in England?

TONY: Yes.

TANIA: Ugh. I'm surprised.

TONY: Don't you have them in Macedonia?

TANIA: Oh yes. I just thought in England – And we certainly have young men who make phone calls in cafes when they could be making be making conversation.

TONY: We've tried that.

TANIA: Could we try again?

TONY: (*Putting down phone.*) If you will be as direct with me as I was with you, we'll have a go at it.

TANIA: All right then. I am here because my father sent me to visit friends till my country grows more peaceful. He chose England for three reasons. One, the Americans, who are also in Macedonia, don't understand us and keep changing sides. Two, the French and Germans understand us but are tired of us. Three, the English, who are occasionally helpful, produced John Constable, whose painting of Willy Lott's Cottage is on many boxes of our biscuits, along with the Boyhood of Raleigh, by someone called Millais, and such pictures speak of peace and hope to my nervous father, and also to me, who am less nervous.

TONY: What I actually meant was, would you like to get to know me personally.

TANIA: I know you already. You are an arrogant seller of rat poison, fixated like your soldiers on casual sex. But you're quite nice to look at.

TONY: Could you go further?

TANIA: You make me nervous. Are you going to report me?

TONY: Of course not. How about we meet later?

TANIA: Well –

(*MATHEW walks in with a cup of coffee.*)

MATHEW: Excuse me – (*Sees phone.*) Oh my God. Are you going to use that thing?

TONY: No.

MATHEW: Then may I – er – all the other tables –

BOTH: Yes.

MATHEW: Thank you. (*Sits, as does TANIA.*) Have I interrupted something?

TANIA: No.

TONY: (*At the same time.*) Yes.

TANIA: We were just talking.

MATHEW: Oh. (*To audience.*) Totty. Not exactly June's idea of company. (*Laughs quietly.*)

TANIA: Who are you talking to?

MATHEW: No-one in particular.

TANIA: To yourself?

MATHEW: No.

TONY: Are you – do you have some medication?

MATHEW: Do you know my niece?

TONY: Not that I –

MATHEW: She says things like that.

TANIA: Are you two connected?

MATHEW/TONY: No.

MATHEW: (*To TANIA.*) If I'm not being impertinent, you don't sound local.

TANIA: I'm a genuine visitor from abroad, with papers, so I'm not living on your social security.

MATHEW: I didn't think you were. (*A kindly smile.*) Do you like England?

TONY: She doesn't come from Austria.

TANIA: You are connected.

MATHEW/TONY: No.

MATHEW: He's from – Bradford?

TANIA: Leeds.

MATHEW: Are you two –

TANIA/TONY: No.

TANIA: I'm from Macedonia.

MATHEW: Oh, I've a wife in Hungary.

TANIA: I'm not surprised. You English are all the same.

MATHEW: And Macedonia is where the mixed vegetables come from.

(*The young couple exchange glances.*)

Macedoines. It's charming really. They're called Macedoines because Macedonia is a multiracial community, or was, or still is, I can't be absolutely sure.

TANIA: (*Pleased.*) Oh it is, it is!

MATHEW: I visited it once and thought it beautiful

TANIA: How wonderful!

TONY: That table's free if you're looking for peace.

TANIA: I'm not.

MATHEW: I'm sorry about the trouble there, but perhaps it will get better.

TANIA: I know it will because it's been so good.

TONY: Isn't anybody taking that table?

MATHEW: You take it if you want.

TONY: No, you.

MATHEW: No, you.

TONY: No, you.

TANIA: You've got work to do.

TONY: Well – (*To TANIA.*) You can join me if you want.

TANIA: I'm happy talking to this gentleman.

MATHEW: Mathew's my name.

TANIA: Mathew. Tony wants to seduce me.

MATHEW: Oh. Shall I –

TONY: Well, actually if you wouldn't mind –

TANIA: No. I prefer his company to yours.

TONY: Well, that's direct. The older man, is it?

TANIA: He knows my country.

TONY: Right. It's your choice. Right. I'll be just over there. Right?

(*TONY leaves. TANIA smiles at MATHEW. He smiles nervously.*)

26

MATHEW: Well – er – erm –

TANIA: You don't often speak to young women, I think.

MATHEW: No, but I did once, and I expect I'll remember how to do it again soon. Was he a nice young man?

TANIA: Not quite.

MATHEW: Would you like to tell me?

TANIA: He tells lies. Do you do that?

MATHEW: Oh no. No.

TANIA: Good.

MATHEW: (*To audience.*) It's hard to know what to say because I am dignified and I can't bring myself to leer and take her home to see my etchings.

TANIA: What are you saying?

MATHEW: I'm expressing helplessness. Tell me, do you ever visit Hungary?

TANIA: Ah, your wife. You have one in Hungary, and one I expect in Romania, and I expect in Czechoslovakia, and I expect in Bosnia, and I expect in Poland. The goatish island race.

MATHEW: I have just the one wife, really, and she lives near Bucharest, no Budapest, no –

TANIA: Don't you know?

MATHEW: She's an English wife who has gone to live in Hungary, where I have been, because there were conferences. I was an academic, but I always confused those names, even though I do know the cities are different.

TANIA: They are in different countries and speak different languages.

MATHEW: Yes, I've been there. (*To audience.*) Well – Faint heart never won fair lady, so – (*is about to speak when:*)

TANIA: I hear you, old man.

MATHEW: I'm not old.

TANIA: Old man is what the English call each other. Hello, old man. How are you, old man. I shot down twenty Messerschmitts, old man. I'm stuck in the past, old man, and long live Winston Churchill.

MATHEW: You are very beautiful and very charming and too nice, I'm sure, to believe outdated views about us English. I wonder if you'd like –

TANIA: Do you really mean what you say about my being beautiful, or are you being polite, or simply hoping for sex?

MATHEW: It doesn't matter, does it. I like saying it, so I'll go on. And I expect you like peace and quiet like the rest of us, so just believe me when I say you are very beautiful, which is anyway what I think, and enjoy my company. You are – beautiful

TANIA: Thank you.

MATHEW: I shall now be bold and try to enter a new life. Would you like lunch?

TANIA: With you?

MATHEW: I'd be happy to take you out, so you could tell me all about why you're in Kew Gardens, and I can tell you why I don't want to do things like teaching people to read. And afterwards, perhaps, we can go for a row on the river. I can still row.

TANIA: Yes, I'll come.

MATHEW: Well – when you've finished your coffee.
(*Enter TONY, without briefcase or phone.*)

TONY: Are you all right?

MATHEW: Yes, she is.

TANIA: Yes.

TONY: There's room at my table, and I thought if you wanted, we could spend a happy half hour discovering what makes us behave so badly to each other. You know?

TANIA: Thank you, but I'm having lunch with this gentleman.

MATHEW: Yes, she really is. So sorry – well, not sorry, but sympathetic.

TONY: You can't mean it.

TANIA: I don't want the rest of my coffee.

MATHEW: Oh well, we'll go then. (*To audience.*) Gosh.
(*To TONY.*) Perhaps we'll meet again, you never know.

TONY: (*As MATHEW and TANIA go.*) How? And how did that happen? How did any of it happen? (*Leaves.*)
(*The scene is being changed as HAROLD, a rather middle-aged young man, appears with a large plastic bin-liner stuffed, we discover, with second-hand clothes.*)

Scene 3

The scene is being changed to a trestle table onto which HAROLD eventually dumps his sack and begins sorting through the clothes. He speaks while the scene is being changed. He is joined by JUNE after a few lines of the speech.

HAROLD: It's really nice at Help The Aged. I've worked in all the others – Scope, the Hospice Shop, Oxfam – and Help The Aged has the nicest goods and the nicest customers. You could say they're rather more up-market in Oxfam – smarter furs, more Ben Sherman shirts, a Gucci shoe or two, scuffed, but not holed, since Richmond is kind to the feet, and their jackets aren't as shiny as we get here. But Oxfam's flashy, always was. Our knick-knacks have a cosier feel, I always think. Not so much stainless steel as you get in Oxfam, and Scope, of course, is more the plaster ducks. But I never quite like the smell of the blouses there, to be honest, Mrs Johnson, nor in the Hospice shop, to be honest again. They don't come so fully washed anywhere as they do to Help The Aged, so you see, there's a feeling of what you might call civilised life about our stock, I always think. What's the matter?

JUNE: I'm trying to see if a walking stick helps you going upstairs. (*She is doing this on the flat floor and looks like a flamingo.*) No, he's better off without it, so we'll sell it here.

HAROLD: The famous Uncle, is it? I've never met him, of course.

JUNE: He can be very spiteful.

HAROLD: Is that why you've kept us apart.?

JUNE: I haven't.

HAROLD: It feels like it.

JUNE: He's a bother, Harold. If he hasn't got something to do he'll get into trouble – sort those out, go on. As if there's not enough already with his wife in Hungary. I tell you, my life is full of anxiety, worry – Idle hands, that's what it is with Uncle Mathew.

HAROLD: Women?

JUNE: Oh no. Though he was prancing around in his stocking feet this morning, getting wet. No, more likely he'll work himself up into depression, they all do, work themselves up, get hypertension, I've seen it, often. They think about their childhoods, what they were like as husbands, what they left unfinished in the world – grief, it's all grief. And then they fall downstairs. Perhaps I should take that back. What d'you think?

HAROLD: You're asking my advice?

JUNE: Yes, I am.

HAROLD: I've never met him so I don't know.

JUNE: He's a retired professor, you know that. And it's Tuesday, shouldn't you be at work?

HAROLD: It's my half day off the buses.

JUNE: That's Wednesdays.

HAROLD: Sometimes it's Wednesdays and sometimes it isn't. When the weather's wet, the rota comes unstuck because people stay off, and it's the ones that know the routes that get called in. Well, I know the routes very well indeed, so I get called in a lot, and so have extra half days to make up for it, like today. I can talk to a professor, I expect.

JUNE: If you were less ambitious for your life we'd get the stock seen to a lot faster. There's someone out there now, shaking the door handle. (*Calls.*) Come back in five minutes! Five – minutes!

HAROLD: There's poetry in me, Mrs Johnson. I thought you'd noticed.

JUNE: Actually, there have been times when, yes, I have noticed. When you've been working over in the window, with the light behind you – But now I'm up to my eyes in real life, and I've no time for poetry. This stuff looks dreadful.

HAROLD: My rhythms express more than my actual words.

JUNE: Once or twice I have wondered what it would be like to travel on your bus.

HAROLD: It would be lovely to have you there, comfy in behind me.

JUNE: I have a fear that I should interrupt you, somehow. Tell you what gear you should be in. People do indicate that that's the sort of thing I do a little bit of. They sort of hint that – I don't know how to put it – that I – that I –

HAROLD: Meddle?

JUNE: No! Well – they do say that I sort of – kind of –

HAROLD: Interfere?

JUNE: What are you getting at?

HAROLD: Nothing.

JUNE: I have no time for interfering.

HAROLD: Anyway, we drivers are safe from all forms of interference. We have a little cubby hole where we sit to do our driving so that we're cut off from the rest of the world. We collect the money, separated from the passengers, and then off we go, shielded by the perspex panel from the general public so that we can follow the route, captains of our ship. The routes, you see, are very difficult and require a lot of concentration.

JUNE: That stuff will have to be passed on, it's horrible. Put it back.

HAROLD: You can be very sharp. This cardigan's lovely.

JUNE: Back. Take it to the Hospice Shop.

HAROLD: Your uncle could be falling downstairs without this stick. I don't know how to put it, but – in future – what would your feelings for him be if – like you said – he were to –

JUNE: Going up and downstairs he uses the banisters.

HAROLD: I've never seen his staircase, as you know.

JUNE: A walking stick gets in the way if you're going up and downstairs, Harold, I've just tried. Do your passengers use a walking stick going upstairs on your bus, or haven't you thought to look? Do you use a walking stick to go up and down stairs? Have you ever gone up and down stairs with anything in your hands and found it anything but a problem? A walking stick gets in the bloody way, and that cardigan is dreadful.

HAROLD: I'm too young to know all that.

JUNE: You need to pull yourself together and think about others.

HAROLD: I help here, don't I?

JUNE: All you do is ponder about which shop has nice smelling blouses. That's not helping. It's something that could get you into trouble.

HAROLD: (*Alarmed.*) It couldn't.

JUNE: I won't tell anyone.

HAROLD: It was just an observation, not a thing I do. I don't do anything at all of that kind.

JUNE: All right, all right.

HAROLD: I just like coming here to tell you things, Mrs Johnson – June. Did you hear? I called you June.

JUNE: Well, it's my name. You must've used it before.

HAROLD: Never. It's a lovely name. Sometimes when I'm driving down beyond Hammersmith Bridge –

JUNE: Harold, you should read the newspapers more. They'd open a whole new world for you. Haven't you really called me June before?

HAROLD: Haven't you noticed? The best part of my life is here at Help The Aged and you haven't noticed that?

JUNE: What are your views on Europe?

HAROLD: (*Unnerved.*) They say Boulogne's very nice.

JUNE: Boulogne? It's odd, but you do have a certain mystic sleepiness about you.

HAROLD: I consider my speech carefully always.

JUNE: The thing about you is that you make one feel warm and soft, and at the same time nervous, like a tepid bath. I'll put this stuff away, while you go and open the door. Go on. (*He leaves and JUNE stuffs the clothes back into the plastic bag, muttering.*) Rubbish. Why do they always give away what they don't want? Why don't they make a real sacrifice and give us things they've just bought? There's never anything I want for myself.

(*HAROLD returns with TONY following him.*)

TONY: Excuse me.

JUNE: Oh. Hello there.

TONY: You've got a picture in the window, The Boyhood of Raleigh.

HAROLD: Very moving.

TONY: I'd like it.

JUNE: Yes, I'm sure you would. And you shall have it. Harold? (*HAROLD goes.*) What else can I do for you, if I may make so bold? (*A little laugh.*)

TONY: You don't have anything by Constable?

JUNE: Not here, at this second, but if you call round at five thirty I could show you one or two in situ. Anything specific?

TONY: Willy Lott's Cottage.

JUNE: Strangely enough, I do believe I can put my hands on that, yes.

TONY: Don't go to any trouble, it's just a whim.

JUNE: The best of life is usually a whim, and there won't be any trouble with this one.

TONY: Well –

(*HAROLD enters.*)

HAROLD: The Boyhood. A lovely piece. Five pounds.

TONY: Right.

JUNE: We'll settle up at five thirty. Just ask for June, if I'm in the back.

HAROLD: Or Mrs Johnson. Five is what we said.

JUNE: And it won't be any trouble to get the Constable.

(*The scene begins to change at this point.*)

TONY: Five thirty then. (*Leaving with the painting.*)

JUNE: (*Calling after him.*) Or quarter past.

HAROLD: (*Anxious.*) Why a constable? It's not the blouses is it?

JUNE: The young gentleman wants a painting by John Constable the artist, and my uncle has one.

HAROLD: (*Taking the plastic bag.*) Oh! I'll help you get it then. We can go together.

JUNE: The young gentleman and I will go alone.

HAROLD: There could have been an accident – depression and no walking stick. You wouldn't want to take the blame alone.

JUNE: Just dump that at the Hospice Shop, or even Oxfam.

HAROLD: I'll be back in time.

JUNE: Will you?

(*JUNE disappears as HAROLD goes on round the stage with his burden.*)

HAROLD: (*Almost singing.*) I'm going to meet a very cultured man. He's very, very clever and I'm going to meet him at last. Oh bliss.

Scene 4

The scene being set is a rowing boat. As HAROLD goes round the stage, MATHEW appears with a bottle of wine, an opener and two glasses, perhaps in a bag, and addresses the audience.

MATHEW: We've had lunch and now it's the river, floating in a dream world where one can choose anything one wants. (*He is now blocking HAROLD's way.*)

HAROLD: Excuse me.

MATHEW: Sorry.

HAROLD: My fault.

MATHEW: Probably.

(*TANIA has now appeared and begins to get into the boat. HAROLD goes on a little and then watches.*)

MATHEW: (*Totters a little, coming rather close.*) Oh haha. Sorry. You sit there. (*He reaches the middle seat.*) Here's a bottle of wine to make the idyll complete. (*He hands it over.*) Ooops. (*A wobble. This time it is a dangerous rather than an erotic event.*) Now. (*He takes the oars and begins to row.*)

HAROLD: Disgusting. (*He goes.*)

MATHEW: Do you know the word idyll?

TANIA: Let's be honest, shall we. Are you thinking about your wife or are you trying to forget her?

MATHEW: Where did you learn your English?

TANIA: Please answer my question.

MATHEW: I am thinking about my wife.

TANIA: Ah.

MATHEW: Just a bit.

TANIA: Nevertheless, I would like to ask –

MATHEW: Do open the bottle.

TANIA: What is the problem with you and your wife?

MATHEW: It wasn't like that. There was a state of affairs, and that is how life is. A state of affairs exists, and then another state of affairs exists. And then another state of affairs, and so on.

TANIA: That isn't how things work.

MATHEW: It is in England.

TANIA: In Macedonia –

MATHEW: Well! *There's* a state of affairs. Oh look, ducks. (*A qucking sound.*)

TANIA: Charming.

MATHEW: And peaceful, don't you think?

TANIA: In Macedonia there was peace for quite a bit of time. But we were only invented quite recently, and so have difficulty knowing what we are. That's why we fight, like people do when they haven't grown together yet. And then there are the oil pipe lines. The different religions. Fear of neighbours, gas pipe lines, Russia and the West. Trade, chiming like a bell, urging competition. Competition encourages racism and fear of neighbours as the money flows backwards and forwards across the mountains between the Black Sea and the Aegean, missing most of us in the middle. And so there's poverty. Nobody competes for that.

MATHEW: The wine will be getting warm.

TANIA: We drank quite a lot at lunch time.

(*MATHEW rests the oars.*)

MATHEW: Tell me about yourself, then.

TANIA: I see. 'Never mind the politics, just tell me your personal problems, darling.'

MATHEW: I wouldn't dream of calling anybody darling, except a cat.

TANIA: The British soldiers always called people –

MATHEW: I'm a pacifist. And you are beautiful Tania.

TANIA: And you are simply Mathew. We will float backwards if you don't row.

MATHEW: Oh. Yes. (*Begins to row.*) My friends used to call me Bunny, actually, years ago. It was ridiculous. Rabbits reproduce like mad, but I never managed it once. (*Stops rowing.*) And rabbits have little fluffy white tails, but on the whole that doesn't have much bearing on it, either.

TANIA: Perhaps it was because inside you're soft and furry.

MATHEW: (*Starts rowing again.*) Oh, I'm not. Oh dear no.

TANIA: So there was anger with your wife?

MATHEW: We've left the ducks completely behind.

TANIA: Was there anger?

MATHEW: Don't condemn me to self-pity.

TANIA: Oh dear.

MATHEW: Self-pity waits all round, and drifts at people like fog, getting into them through somewhere like the back of the neck, and spreading into all the creases , a coating of glue.

TANIA: Ugh. I'd rather not talk about it.

MATHEW: People shrivel with it. You could say it's the opposite of sexual excitement, which, as I suppose you know, produces an instant change in – I mean – the opposite of shrivel – (*Stops rowing, oars up out of the water.*) It gets embarrassing for men to stand up. And they can't help it. A pretty face appears, or something very – and woosh. Nothing anyone can do about it. Well, self-pity is exactly the same but in reverse. (*Starts rowing.*) There is a person, happy as if all the world was pretty people, pretty, pretty people of all sorts – all – all – laughing and chattering and quite liking one, till suddenly – (*Stops rowing, oars down in the water.*) oh Jesus – a slip of the tongue, a distorted memory, and the fog-snake slips and slobbers into you, and nibbles and releases his sticky poison. And then the world detaches itself, slips away, over there, into a far off view, everyone walking about as themselves, while here – insidious treacle, sweet and horrid. We love it, you see. Once started, we can't get enough. The world spins away while we melt in warm self-pity, and I could weep for that. (*The ducks quack again.*)

TANIA: Keep rowing.

(*He does but it is an effort.*)

MATHEW: It is a ridiculous phenomenon. But we are ridiculous. From time to time I do decide that ridiculous is a virtue, a place we belong in, the definitive good. Ridiculous means happy.

TANIA: Would you like me to row?

MATHEW: No, of course not.

TANIA: Are you sure?

MATHEW: Of course I'm sure. This is my idyll.

TANIA: A rather gloomy idyll.

MATHEW: Oh – isolation.

TANIA: What?

MATHEW: There are unsocial moments when you want to be understood, and instead –

TANIA: As an older man speaking to a young girl you shouldn't try saying you want to be understood. It's a complete turn off.

MATHEW: I was just making a general observation about how impossible it is to make the things one says mean-ingful. It's unimportant, and if it hurts too much one can always take up golf. It's surprising what you can be driven to in bad moments.

TANIA: We don't play golf in Eastern Europe.

MATHEW: It might stop you fighting. (*Rowing slows.*)
The current seems less strong here.

TANIA: Do you often take young girls for idylls?

MATHEW: My niece says I should take up teaching.

TANIA: You'd scare the children to death.

MATHEW: (*Stops rowing, alarmed.*) Am I scary?

TANIA: A bit.

MATHEW: Oh. Shall I open the bottle or will you?

TANIA: All right. You. (*She hands him the bottle and the cork-screw. He stands to open the bottle and wobbles.*) Don't sink us.

MATHEW: No. Success (*The bottle is open.*) Glasses.
(*She hands them to him from the bag, he fills both.*)
Here we are. (*He hands her a glass.*) Steady.
(*They wobble and it looks as if he is going to kiss her.*)

TANIA: We're going backwards.

MATHEW: Oh. Can you hold this?
(*He hands her the bottle. Their hands touch rather too long.*)

TANIA: Let go of it.

MATHEW: Oh. Yes. And here's my glass.
(*Still seated, she puts the bottle between her knees and takes his glass.*)
You're in what could be called a helpless position.

TANIA: What are you thinking of doing?

MATHEW: What I'm thinking of doing is – well –
(*The ducks quack.*)
I mean I want to be thought a gentleman, though
obviously – D'you know the word randy?

TANIA: Yes. The soldiers were randy. And you're a pacifist.
See, the ducks.

MATHEW: Oh. Ooops. (*Sits and rows. To audience.*) I rather
wish you hadn't seen that.

TANIA: Who are you talking to?

MATHEW: Other people. Why did you quarrel with Tony.

TANIA: He made me nervous, and I'm worried enough about
home. Bye bye, ducks.

MATHEW: Are you more nervous of me than you are of him?

TANIA: I am now, a bit. If you ask someone if they're nervous of you they become nervous automatically.

MATHEW: Oh.

TANIA: I like you, provided you don't try to kiss me.

MATHEW: Oh.

TANIA: Perhaps after this we'd better say goodbye.

MATHEW: I suppose we better had, if that's how we feel.

TANIA: How do you feel?

MATHEW: Rather nervous of myself, actually. (*Stops rowing.*)
I'm not mad, am I?

TANIA: You could be. Tony and I both thought you were.

MATHEW: You talked about it?

TANIA: With our eyes. Does that upset you?

MATHEW: I just – surprisingly- slightly wish I hadn't met
you. I'm going to pull in to the bank.

TANIA: So we can drink together before – or in case – I walk
away.

MATHEW: I must say you're unusual.

TANIA: There's nothing wrong with me, except for worry about
my country. You've never had to leave yours, have you.

MATHEW: No. There. No current here by the shore. (*He has
stopped rowing.*) So, where are you staying?

TANIA: With some friends.

MATHEW: Where?

TANIA: Is that your business?

MATHEW: I'd forgotten your paranoia about policemen.
(*TANIA hands him his drink.*)
Thank you. Cheers.

TANIA: If you want to know, I'm with family friends in St
John's Wood, and they said it would be nice if I came here,
on my own, to see a different place. I can't think why they
said it, except that they were tired of me. I was complaining
they had abandoned our country at a time when it needed
them, and my friends said 'Really? Go to Richmond.' I
have to say I haven't received any insights in Richmond.

MATHEW: I had a passionate affair once, and I rather think it
happened in St John's Wood. One does forget things.
I can't remember anything about it now, not even the girl's
name. All blank, no insights… No! Not true! Her name
was Hermione! Good old Hermione, face like a bass fiddle.
Actually, I'm not mad. I'm dreadfully harmless.

TANIA: No-one's harmless.

MATHEW: Perhaps. Come on, let's go and sit on the grass, and you can tell me everything you want to about home.

TANIA: I'm supposed to go back to tell my friends about Kew Gardens.

MATHEW: It's all trees.

TANIA: And I don't know if I want to be alone with you any more.

MATHEW: There are lots of others sitting down up there. Give me the bottle.

TANIA: All right. (*She does so. They are both now standing facing each other. He has a glass and the bottle. She has her own glass.*) Oops!

(*He steadies her. She smiles. He slowly moves forward. She doesn't move. He kisses her gently on the lips without putting his arms round her. He breaks the kiss.*)

MATHEW: Well?

TANIA: You're right. You're harmless.

(*He leans a little more forcefully. But she puts her hand out to stop him.*)

TANIA: No, that would be scary.

MATHEW: There's something awfully experienced about you, isn't there.

TANIA: Does that scare you?

MATHEW: No, it doesn't.

TANIA: (*Getting out of the boat.*) Let's sit on the grass, then, and drink wine and not have any more sex. I will trust you, because actually, to be honest, I'm lonely. (*Leaves.*)

MATHEW: I wouldn't trust me too far, then, because so am I.

(*The ducks can be heard off going 'quack, quack quack'.*)

(*Irritated.*) Oh shut up! (*He follows TANIA off.*)

(*The scene begins to be changed back to the patio. JUNE with the stick and HAROLD and TONY, carrying the 'Boyhood of Raleigh' enter as the scene changes, and walk round eventually arriving at the patio. They speak as they go.*)

TONY: Are you sure it's no trouble?

HAROLD: Of course not.

JUNE: He spoke to me and there's no need for you to come at all.

HAROLD: I want to.

TONY: I'm feeling rather silly now, anyway.

HAROLD: It's the fulfilment of a dream, and a collision of symbolic forces, if I can put it that way. 'There's a divinity that shapes our ends, rough hew them how we will.'

TONY: You talk a lot, don't you?

JUNE: A lot of rubbish. Now, the old boy can be facetious so be prepared. And here we are. On the patio, England, home and beauty.

Scene 5

Enter JUNE, with the stick, HAROLD and TONY. TONY carries his briefcase and the print of the 'Boyhood of Raleigh'.

HAROLD: Oh! Oh! What beauties!

TONY: It's only a patio.

HAROLD: It's the patio. And is that a rose tree?

JUNE: Leave it alone, it's been treated. Uncle? He's usually sitting out here. Uncle!

HAROLD: P'raps he's lying at the foot of the staircase.

JUNE: Rubbish. We passed there and he wasn't. Is he in the bushes?

HAROLD: More likely on the upstairs landing.

JUNE: You're not going up there, he could be in his bath. Uncle? (*She goes back into the house.*)

TONY: I shouldn't be here at all.

HAROLD: She'll find your picture when she's settled. Willy Lott's Cottage, ever so evocative. I have visited galleries, you know.

TONY: The stupid thing is, I probably won't need it. I'll never meet the girl again, and anyway she's Macedonian.

HAROLD: Don't they need visas?

TONY: Probably. Why d'you want to come to this place so much?

HAROLD: Well! He's so distinguished, a professor and everything. To use a somewhat overblown word, it's awe inspiring to be actually present, inside his head, as it were. It's difficult to get inside my own quite often. Would you know why there are so few buds on this?

TONY: I hope she's quick with the picture because I've got things to do.

HAROLD: At a quarter to six? That's what I call the vacant time of day, unless you've got a home, and even then, half past five has more urgency about it.

TONY: I can wait.

HAROLD: Will the picture become a talisman if you never meet again?

TONY: No. I don't like Constable, nor Millais.

HAROLD: Oh, I always think The Boyhood's full of calm, and hope for the future.

TONY: Got a lot of that, have you?

HAROLD: Yes.

TONY: Not promising, exactly

HAROLD: If I can be honest, Tony, I don't find you immensely sympathetic.

TONY: I'm sympathetic. You have to be, selling rat poison. What's all this about falling down stairs?

HAROLD: It's another strand in Mrs Johnson's drama of life. To be honest, it's a rather painful drama, in my opinion, based as it is on a blood relationship, and those, of course, are always inclined to be sharp, to use a word of many meanings.

TONY: I wouldn't know.

HAROLD: Nevertheless, she thinks very highly of Uncle Mathew. It's not for me to say, but I think you can sense some things about him from what I might call the ambience.

TONY: No.

HAROLD: I am surprised. Those of us who are intuitive can feel a kind of cultured aura that is, as the French might put it, *je ne sais* –
(*Enter JUNE with Willy Lott and without the walking stick.*)

JUNE: He's not here, so he must be all right. And here's the picture, young man.

TONY: But it's his.

JUNE: He's almost certainly going to give it to the shop, so price it, Harold.

HAROLD: (*Taking it.*) Well, a Constable, with good edges and just a slight coffee stain on the dog, that's quite a bargain.

MATHEW: (*Off.*) Hullo!

JUNE: Uncle?

MATHEW: (*Off.*) Who's been sitting in my chair?

JUNE: Did either of you sit in a chair while I was upstairs looking?

HAROLD: When we passed the ottomman in the hall I did venture –

JUNE: He said chair.

TONY: It's the three bears.

JUNE: What bears?

TONY: It's what they said when they thought that Goldilocks had –

MATHEW: (*Off.*) Who's been eating my porridge?

JUNE: He never touches porridge. It's muesli, though I've told him about prunes. How much Harold, go on?

HAROLD: I think another fiver should cover it.

TONY: I don't want to do this, coming into a strange man's house and –

JUNE: He's not strange, he's quite sensible when he wants to be. That'll be ten, my love, and I'm sure you'd like a sherry when he offers.

MATHEW: (*Off.*) Who's been sleeping in my bed?

(*Giggles from MATHEW and TANIA.*)

JUNE: Bed?

TONY: He's been at the bottle.

HAROLD: Ten pounds altogether.

JUNE: My uncle is not a drunk.

HAROLD: Perhaps it's the wet socks gone to his head.

TONY: That sounds suggestive. (*Light laugh.*)

MATHEW: (*Off, with TANIA.*) Who's been sleeping in my bed, who's been sleeping in my bed! (*Giggles.*)

JUNE: He's got a woman. You know what that means.

TONY: I don't think I should stay.

JUNE: Oh yes. Witnesses. He'll be changing his will before we know where we are, leaving everything to some hussey.

(*Enter MATHEW and TANIA.*)

MATHEW: Ah. Company.

TANIA: Tony!

TONY: Tania?

MATHEW: Welcome, mobile phone man. And welcome
June, welcome everyone to my patio where I am at peace.

HAROLD: Oh dear.

JUNE: You are drunk.

TANIA: (*To TONY.*) What are you doing here?

TONY: I've bought you a present. You said you liked it.

TANIA: Oh how sweet.

MATHEW: I'm in a state of heightened consciousness and
very good manners. (*To HAROLD.*) Good evening. Have
we met?

HAROLD: Well, in a way.

MATHEW: Either we have or we haven't.

HAROLD: I bumped into you this afternoon, with a plastic
bin-liner.

JUNE: You never said.

MATHEW: I never had a plastic bin liner, so it must've been
someone else.

HAROLD: No, you were – he was – what you might call
occupied. But I'm very honoured to be here. Sir.
Whatever happens.

JUNE: (*To TONY about MATHEW.*) Do you two know each other?

TONY: We've met.

HAROLD: Is that the girl?

TONY: Yes.

HAROLD: Oh dear, oh dear.

TONY: Why?

HAROLD: Nothing.

JUNE: Is someone making a fool of me?

MATHEW: Impossible.

HAROLD: It's fate, anyway. And he's bought you lovely
pictures which I like even if he doesn't

JUNE: Don't intervene, Harold. My uncle's unwell. (*To
TANIA.*) And you've been with him?

TANIA: I think I should explain –

MATHEW: He has a mobile phone.

JUNE: Who does?

MATHEW: He does, and I shall sit down (*Does so.*) (*To HAR-
OLD.*) This is my house, you know.

HAROLD: And a wonderful place it is.

MATHEW: Yes, isn't it.

HAROLD: Here. (*Pulls out chair for him.*)

JUNE: And don't go leaving it to anyone else. Who exactly are you?

TANIA: I come from Macedonia.

MATHEW: Like Alexander the Great.

JUNE: He was perverted of course.

TANIA: That was a different Macedonia.

JUNE: Are you ashamed of him?

MATHEW: June's my niece, and objects to anything she can't experience herself. I imagine that Alexander would have felt the same way about her.

HAROLD: There's ten pounds owing to us, June.

TONY: Here.

JUNE: Do you all know each other?

MATHEW: We had coffee in Kew Gardens. Who is he?
    (*Reference to HAROLD.*)

HAROLD: I'm an assistant at Help the Aged. Here's the picture.
    (*TONY now has both pictures.*)

MATHEW: You look as if you want the lavatory.

HAROLD: I don't. It's just the modest way I stand sometimes.

MATHEW: And what's he doing with my Willy Lott's Cottage?

JUNE: It's the shop's. You don't want it, it hasn't hung up for years.

MATHEW: Hetty gave it to me, and it has sentimental value.

JUNE: Don't harp on about Aunt Hetty. Is she staying?

MATHEW: Like the rest of you, she's welcome to be part of the evening's company.

JUNE: What company? No-one's told me anything.

TANIA: I'm Tania, from Macedonia, sexually straight, and Tony's bought the pictures for me, haven't you, to persuade me he's a serious person.

TONY: It's a stupid gesture, especially as I don't much care for them. But since I've done it, will you have dinner with me?

TANIA: Yes.

MATHEW: What?

HAROLD: Oh – oh –

MATHEW: I asked her to eat here. She said she would.
(*To HAROLD.*) Did you steal those pictures?

HAROLD: No! I'm a bus driver.

MATHEW: Have you parked outside? Because there's not a
lot of room down these little streets and a parked bus –

JUNE: Pull yourself together, Uncle, and let's be clear about
things. You can't invite strange foreigners into your house
for dinner.

MATHEW: She's not strange, she's very sensible, and she is
staying.

JUNE: She's not because we don't know if she has papers.

TANIA: Are you a policewoman?

JUNE: No, I'm a Christian.

MATHEW: She has a visa and you're not to mention that
again, because we know she has a visa, and what's more,
we like her.

HAROLD: Oh –

JUNE: You've got the dithers.

MATHEW: I have not!

JUNE: Yes you have.

MATHEW: Shut up!

TANIA: I think I want to go with Tony for a meal.

MATHEW: Oh – You could both stay if you wanted.

TANIA: He has bought me these pictures. He means to
be serious. I like that, because he's nice looking and –
However, he does say he's a liar, and that he really wants
to do what the British army calls get into my knickers.

JUNE: Your knickers?

MATHEW: I expect you want to get into his, too. They don't
exactly look harmless to me.

TONY: I don't think I want to hang around listening to family
rows.

TANIA: It's very childish of you to say things like that, Bunny.

TONY: Bunny? He's called Bunny?

JUNE: No he's not. He's a responsible retired professor, and
no-one would dream of demeaning him with a name like
that. Now, you've got your pictures, we've got our ten
pounds, Harold's going home, so you can go and leave us
alone. Though Tony might enjoy an evening on the patio
making interesting conversation.

HAROLD: I don't want to go home.

TONY: Bunny. What were you two up to?

TANIA: Nothing. I'm sorry, Mathew. I would like to stay for dinner because – and I know I said I would and things but – I didn't know –

MATHEW: (*Cold.*) Goodnight.

TANIA: Goodnight. Thank you for our conversation.

HAROLD: You've had conversation with him?

TANIA: And that's all.

HAROLD: All? I've wanted conversation with him for years, and you just climb into a boat with him and – Oh! Foreigners.

TONY: A boat?

TANIA: Mathew?

MATHEW: I've said goodnight.

(*TANIA and TONY leave.*)

TONY: (*As they leave.*) What sort of boat?

TANIA: A rowing boat.

TONY: (*They are off.*) The old bugger.

JUNE: Oh dear. That boy and I were just getting friendly. Still, he's taken her away from you, and that's something.

HAROLD: It was meant, really, the two of them.

MATHEW: Who by?

HAROLD: Well, you know. Fate.

MATHEW: I hope I never have to go on your bus if you leave the route it travels up to fate. Incidentally, I do think you should remove it from –

HAROLD: I haven't got a bus!

MATHEW: Then you aren't a bus driver!

HAROLD: I am!

JUNE: Now, now. We can have a nice quiet time together, discussing your job while Harold fetches the stick before he goes. Go on. We've had enough scares this evening, not finding him and wondering.

HAROLD: But he's all right.

MATHEW: I do not want a stick, and Tania says I'd scare children if I taught.

JUNE: She's really got to you, hasn't she.

MATHEW: Are you called Harold?

HAROLD: Yes.

MATHEW: We had a king called that, once, a real loser. Are you consorting with my niece? Doing your bit for charity?

HAROLD: I am not.

MATHEW: I don't suppose she'd notice if you were.

JUNE: I would. The company of men is something I very much enjoy. And you obviously need something to keep you occupied, Uncle.

MATHEW: Why did you let them go? You could've been nice, instead of talking about papers.

JUNE: Well, they're coming in everywhere, her sort. We've had to sell the marmalade from the W.I. stall at Help The Aged, because it doesn't go any more. People's breakfast habits are changing – ham, cheese, yoghurty stuff, continental breakfasts creeping across the channel, you don't know what's happening, sitting here. The British breakfast isn't safe.

MATHEW: It isn't healthy.

HAROLD: Isn't it?

JUNE: Of course it is. She's bewitched you, hasn't she. Scaring the children, a nice old thing like you. She's after your money.

MATHEW: I've made my will and you'll get lucky, June. Though selling that print we had to cover the stain where Hetty threw a cup of coffee at the wall – I might just alter things.

HAROLD: Was she violent?

JUNE: Of course not. This is Richmond. And don't you dare alter anything after all I've done for you.

MATHEW: We were going to have a party.

HAROLD: I found him rather sharp.

JUNE: I thought him sophisticated. She was pretty coarse, with that soldiers talk about – you know. I'll get the sherry.

HAROLD: No, let me.

JUNE: I'll do it, you find the stick.

HAROLD: I'd get more pleasure from the sherry.

(*As they reach the exit, TANIA comes back followed by TONY without the paintings.*)

JUNE: Oh!

TANIA: I'd like to stay after all.

MATHEW: Ah. Would you. Why's that? Or perhaps it was just meant, eh, Harold?

HAROLD: Well, 'There's a divinity that shapes – '

MATHEW: Bollocks. Do you both want to stay?

TONY: (*Surly.*) Yes. Definitely. Bunny.

JUNE: Where are the pictures?

TANIA: Disappointingly, he needed his hands free before I was ready.

HAROLD: Why ?

JUNE: Harold, I wonder if you're too young to stay for dinner with the rest of us?

HAROLD: Oh. I see. Hands, yes.

JUNE: Go and find the stick.

MATHEW: Well, well. The mistiming of youth. That makes me feel a bit triumphant, so if you don't mind – (*He takes his shoes off.*)

TONY: Oh, the wet socks.

JUNE: You'll catch your death.

MATHEW: I won't.

JUNE: Those who look after themselves –

MATHEW: I will not catch cold!

TANIA: Bunny.

MATHEW: She sets me on.

HAROLD: I'm sure she doesn't, nice kind lady.

MATHEW: Oh. Just come and look at this rose tree, Harold. (*Drags him over.*) What do you normally find on a rose tree at this time of year?

HAROLD: Buds. I said, didn't I.

MATHEW: They were there this morning, flourishing away, and then June came bursting in all over, Helping the Aged, and cut them off like Delilah going at Samson, and she threw the buds, like the heads of traitors, into the dustbin. How's that for an act of vandalism?

HAROLD: Perhaps it was pruning.

JUNE: Yes.

MATHEW: It was viciousness.

TANIA: It's only a rose.

MATHEW: Like you, a thing of beauty and a joy for ever.

TANIA: There's something awful in the way you all use words. You sound so isolated. You have jobs and homes

and buses and trains and cars and roads and shops and
money and gardens, and the way you speak is so full of
all that. You don't know what it's like to live on the brink,
always afraid, not knowing what's happening around you.
I live on the edge of Europe where some of the villages are
like jungle villages. Nothing in them you would recognise.
And people fight over them. People shell them. They kill.
How can you be angry over a rose tree?

JUNE: I know what villages are. I've been to Stowe-on-the
Wold. People live in them because it's healthier than
London and they force up the price of houses. You needn't
tell me about villages.

TANIA: In our villages you have to shit at the bottom of the
garden in an old hut beside a lot of turkeys, and there's
nothing but mud.

JUNE: We don't want to know.

HAROLD: Why turkeys?

TANIA: Because they make good watch dogs. However, they
do tell every one when you've gone down there to –

JUNE: Don't ask embarrassing questions, Harold. You can be
very clumsy socially.

MATHEW: Oh God. I offended very deeply, didn't I.

TANIA: Yes.

MATHEW: I am so sorry. It was one of those catastrophic
moments when one doesn't think, and simply gets carried
away with rage. Oh hell! Of course my roses don't matter.

TANIA: It's all right.

MATHEW: No, it isn't. But I'll – The meal will be lovely.
It will take a little time, as I wasn't prepared for company.
(*Anxious.*) But I love it, love it now it's here. (*Begins to move off.*)

TONY: (*Acid.*) What was so wrong with trying to kiss you, then?

TANIA: It was a move too soon.

TONY: Really?

TANIA: Yes. Island people are always unsophisticated because
they have no-one to argue with except themselves. In Europe, we get invaded and bombed and killed and that's a
great education, which teaches us to know the proper time
for anything, including the moment you can take a girl in
your arms.

MATHEW: I know the moment.

TONY: Oh, do you. What exactly did you do in that boat?

TANIA: It was private.

TONY: I've spent half the day finding special presents for you, so I think I have a right to know what you were doing with an old lecher in a rowing boat.

TANIA: You haven't bought me, Tony.

TONY: No, but I might expect to be told the truth, especially as you're so bloody keen on others telling it.

TANIA: I don't know if I want you to stay for dinner.

MATHEW: Oh you do, you do. It will be good. I promise I'll behave, and not offend you again, in any way, even though you look so unbearably – enfoldable. Please, let's just enjoy one another over a good meal. I'll try to be gentle, and I'll cook it; June will be kind and welcoming; Tony will be patient and loving; Tania will relax and smile, and Harold – (*Can't resist slipping into irony.*) Harold will speak poetry about the working classes.

HAROLD: I won't.

MATHEW: And so we'll have good company for the evening, with each other's more interesting selves, and that will bring peace.

HAROLD: I don't think you realise that I want culture, not a discussion of the working classes.

MATHEW: Now for the kitchen, and simple food. (*To audience.*) I do mean all that, I think I mean all that, and I know so well that I want it. It's the first spontaneous company in fifteen years.

TANIA: Who do you talk to?

MATHEW: People, come to see our celebration of peace and calm. June, I think you've got the dithers.

JUNE: I have not!

MATHEW: Well, try to hold them back, because I've decided to forgive you for the buds. Heigh ho, let's hope for the best. (*Leaves for the kitchen.*)

JUNE: It was pruning.

TONY: He lusts after you, as much as I do.

TANIA: He's kind, Tony.

JUNE: (*To TONY.*) And so am I. Just remember that.

End of Act One.

ACT TWO

Scene 1

The table has a cloth on it and a tray of cutlery. TONY looks towards the kitchen. HAROLD brings in an unlit candelabra and tries to strike matches to light the candles.

TONY: Helping him cook. I've heard it call some funny things, but cooking –

HAROLD: They are cooking. June's with them, so relax. (*Match fails.*) Occasionally I entertain my colleagues to evenings of good food and interesting conversation. (*Match fails as before.*) I don't of course run to a patio, but I have a pleasant sitting room/dining room – a through room supported by an RSJ decorated in eau de nil – and I, too, have candles. (*Match fails.*) No, I'll manage. Of course, there aren't a great many bus drivers who live in Richmond, but my colleagues from the other parts of the metropolis do enjoy an exotic evening out and – (*Match fails again. Irritated TONY moves in quickly with a lighter.*) I'll manage!

TONY: You won't!

HAROLD: I will!

TONY: For Christ's sake! There! (*Candles lit.*)

HAROLD: Quite took the edge off my little ritual. Have you got any further yourself?

TONY: Pardon?

HAROLD: With the Yugoslav.

TONY: She's Macedonian.

HAROLD: Same thing.

TONY: If you can tell the difference between bus drivers in Richmond and bus drivers from other parts of the metropolis, I should think you could bring yourself to notice the difference between –

HAROLD: Do you mean to spoil things?

TONY: What is there to spoil?

HAROLD: The individuality of the event. It's very special. The patio, the candles, the table, the wise old man –

TONY: Hah.

HAROLD: I'm here tonight because I've been placed here by the Great Game, played by Eternal Spirits who toy with us in the Great Ether. To be honest, I feel this is my spiritual home, which I've been selected for and finally moved to.

TONY: Bloody hell. Who by?

HAROLD: The Great Player.

TONY: God?

HAROLD: Life is all a game, Tony, gently, irresistibly played by Who Knows What.

TONY: What would you do if Mathew came in and said, 'All right, Harold, you can go now'?

HAROLD: I'd go, of course. I would've been expelled from paradise for some unknown defect, and so would experience what the books I read call spiritual dysfunction.

TONY: Well, let's hope he remembers who you are and takes a fancy to you.

HAROLD: A what?

TONY: Likes you. Are you –

HAROLD: No.

TONY: It doesn't worry me.

HAROLD: Never mind you. Some decisions I try to make for myself. I shall now ask June about the napiery.

TONY: The what?

HAROLD: Serviettes. (*He heads for the kitchen exit as JUNE enters.*)

JUNE: Right, Harold, get in the kitchen and keep an eye on those two. They're very close. No, Tony, you stay here. Pretend to look for the sherry, Harold, and don't find it till I call you.

HAROLD: There, you see? Responsibility and preferment. (*He goes.*)

TONY: Is he mauling her?

JUNE: Tony, since we're here together for the evening, I have to say you're what I would call a downright stunning good looker.

TONY: Thank you, Mrs Johnson, but I'd like to know what's –

JUNE: (*Possibly holding him by the lapel as he moves.*) And you'll notice that I'm in pretty good shape myself, as a matter of actual fact.

TONY: You may have noticed I am here because of Tania.

JUNE: That's just puppy love, not mature passion. And any way she's foreign.

TONY: Let's not misunderstand each other –

JUNE: Sit down. Sit. I'm not going to be coarse, just practical. Think football. The young unfledged player is always rushing about like a child, booting the ball all over the field, not paying attention, can't see the goal mouth for boyish enthusiasm. The older player weaves and ducks, and keeps his brain going, using skills – oh skills, skills – skills learnt from many a long season on the pitch, and all the time he's taking time, exploring, manoeuvring, moving gracefully and never hurrying, and all the while he has an eye – or an ear, or a sixth sense – on the mouth of that goal, drawing towards it as he plays for it like an angler plays a fish – oh, the hook – and he feints for it, crosses past it, darts back and passes here and there before recovering, and then, half facing it, and measuring his energy against the distance to be covered, his angle against the uprights and crossbar, he swirls round and with the deftest little flick that brings the whole stadium to its feet howling with cheers, and pushing sweat to stand like jewels on his forehead, he smashes it in, unstoppable and oh so beautiful. And we know where he learnt all that. From players with experience, those who caress the game as if it were a statue, a work of high art. Have you seen them doing that, the experienced ones, on Match of the Day?

TONY: Match of the Day has never seemed quite like that to me, Mrs Johnson.

JUNE: I'll take you to a football match, Tony. Teach you to dribble.

TONY: What happened to Mr Johnson?

JUNE: We don't ask that question. So what are we doing after I get Uncle Mathew to bed?

TONY: I'm going to discuss the Macedonian question.

JUNE: Don't waste yourself on impossibilities. I'll be here all evening, and I'm very possible indeed.

TONY: You wouldn't mind leaving your uncle a prey to Tania?

JUNE: Of course I'd mind. (*To off.*) Harold! (*To TONY.*) But I
can keep more than one ball in the air at a time. (*To off.*)
What are they doing?

TONY: You care more about what they're doing than what
you could do with me. (*Peering, like she is.*) What are they
doing?

JUNE: (*Low voiced.*) I could give you frontal sex, anal sex, oral
sex, any other sex you choose to think of, and could do it
twenty four hours a day.

TONY: I'm a working lad, June.

JUNE: You're leading me on.

TONY: He's proposing.

JUNE: What? I'd better go in. No, that's meddling, and you sit
down. Harold! (*To TONY.*) I want to have things settled not
always jumping about.

HAROLD: (*Off.*) Yes?

JUNE: We want sherry.

(*HAROLD enters with napkins and salt and pepper and
things.*)

HAROLD: You said pretend about the sherry.

TONY: What d'you mean, settled?

JUNE: I always seem to be on the move, and tonight could be
an oasis of complete physical satisfaction.

HAROLD: What?

JUNE: You didn't hear that. What are they doing?

HAROLD: She's talking about a town I can't pronounce, and
he's too busy cooking to listen.

JUNE: I better go in and see before she pounces. I'll get the
sherry. It's always down to mugsy here.

HAROLD: What did you mean when you said the thing I
didn't hear?

TONY: She wants to play football with me.

HAROLD: She's never wanted to play that with me.

JUNE: (*Popping back as she goes.*) You don't want to touch him,
Harold.

HAROLD: I wouldn't dream –

JUNE: You know what we'd think at Help The Aged if you
did. What with the blouses. And where's the walking stick?
(*She goes.*)

HAROLD: I wish people wouldn't tell me what I want.

TONY: You don't want me, though, do you?

HAROLD: No.

TONY: Good, because I want Tania, and I feel pretty urgent about it. Possibly dangerous. June's not my sort, you know.

HAROLD: (*Cynical.*) Football.

TONY: Shall I help you with that?

(*HAROLD is laying the table.*)

HAROLD: Don't suck up to me.

TONY: I'm not. And I'm very sorry if I –

HAROLD: I'm not pathetic, you know.

TONY: No, of course you're not.

HAROLD: You're lying.

TONY: I'm not. It's dreadful to suggest you're pathetic.

HAROLD: Go away. Right away. You're spoiling things.

TONY: I'm simply here because of Tania.

HAROLD: The rest of us are here for a cultural evening of joy.

(*Enter JUNE carrying a tray of sherry and glasses and tucked under her arm are the two prints.*)

JUNE: All right, Harold, you can go now.

HAROLD: What?

JUNE: And pour me a glass of sherry before you do. She's coming out here.

TONY: You don't mean he can go.

JUNE: Yes, I do.

TONY: And then come back? There are five places.

JUNE: Of course he'll come back. I only want him to find where he's put the walking stick.

HAROLD: Oh the relief.

JUNE: Did you touch him?

HAROLD: No!

JUNE: Then sherry, come on. (*Of the prints.*) I've brought these out so she won't forget them when she goes.

TONY: She won't go without me.

HAROLD: Sherry, dry as silk. (*He pours and hands round sherry during the following.*)

JUNE: Tania!

TONY: What are you up to?

JUNE: She said she was coming out. Though if you want her to leave us alone – find the stick, Harold.

HAROLD: I'm doing the sherry.

TONY: I don't want any more suggestive conversation about sex.

JUNE: Did you have that with Harold?

TONY: No.

HAROLD: Was it you he had it with?

JUNE: He's one of us.

HAROLD: But you never talk about sex with me.

JUNE: I don't want it with you.

HAROLD: I don't want it with you, but we could talk about it. I'm your friend!

JUNE: It's no use talking to Harold about sex. His rhythms won't handle it.

HAROLD: Our rhythms fit very well and we can talk about anything.

JUNE: But not everything.

HAROLD: Yes, everything. I was really looking forward to tonight, moving into realms of literature and art that bus routes aren't always open to.

JUNE: If I'm not mistaken, Harold, this afternoon I used the phrase poetry in motion about you, and that'll do about that and everything connected with it. Are those olives? (*TONY has picked a bowl and is about to hand them round.*)

HAROLD: There were only crisps.

JUNE: (*Taking one.*) They're so noisy. Get the stick, will you?

HAROLD: In a minute.

JUNE: He has to know he's old and past it, and so does she, and that the proper cure for being lonely is to do a job of work.

HAROLD: And you don't want blaming if he breaks his neck.

JUNE: No, so get that stick.

TONY: The symbol of his decrepitude.

HAROLD: In a minute. (*They munch crisps and drink sherry.*) To be honest, I prefer sweet sherry, but your supposed to like it dry, so –

JUNE: Don't pretend to be an independent spirit.

HAROLD: I am, sometimes.

JUNE: Oh, you drive your bus beautifully, but you'd no more take off to the coast with it one day, full of angry passengers expecting Shepherd's Bush, than fly to the moon, Tania!

HAROLD: Of course not.

TONY: Reliable bus drivers are important.

HAROLD: Oh! If you could hear yourself. Oh! You think you're so superior saying any old thing that comes into your head.

JUNE: D'you want to put an axe in it?

HAROLD: Yes.

TONY: I'll go and see what's happening.

JUNE: I'll go.

TONY: I'll go.

JUNE: You stay exactly where you are, outlined by the candlelight, and I'll check that they're still safe.

TONY: I really don't know why I stay.

HAROLD: You stay because we're wonderful.

JUNE: You get that stick. Tania! (*JUNE heads for the exit as TANIA enters.*)

TANIA: June, your uncle is the very nicest man in the world.

JUNE: He's not.

TONY: He's old.

TANIA: He's calm, he's amusing, and he listens.

TONY: He's cranky and lecherous –

JUNE: And impotent.

HAROLD: How d'you know that? You're his niece. Aren't you?

JUNE: Of course I am. All right, I don't know it, but he could be.

TANIA: He's not.

TONY: How do you know?

TANIA: I saw it in the boat.

TONY: Playing bunnies? Let's go.

TANIA: He told me that when he and Mrs Hetty threw things at each other they always missed on purpose. Once they hit the postman, both at the same time.

JUNE: Impossible.

TANIA: It was summer, the door was open and they were circling round. He's just so kind. I'm staying.

TONY: He threw things at his wife.

TANIA: He's very truthful. Why did you cut the buds from his rose tree?

JUNE: They were out of control. And pruning is a good metaphor for life.

TONY: Not football? Look. I intend to say something straightforward and convincing. I tell you here, calmly, and
honestly, that I want to take you in my arms and kiss you.
Now. Properly. Warmly. To hold you. To brush my lips on
your skin. To touch your hair, and your neck, and, without
getting into your knickers, to relax into the warmth of –

JUNE: Just a minute!

HAROLD: I should think so.

JUNE: You're in company, and this is my uncle's house, and I
decide on the boundaries.

TONY: I'd like to say I love her, but that's a thing people
often say when they run out of conversation. However, it
does seem to me quite likely that I do love you, and I'd
like you to believe me when I say that at least I think I do.

HAROLD: There's a dangerous whiff of liberty in the air.

TONY: I've said it in this rather starchy way because then it
sounds more truthful, and I know you have a thing about
that.

TANIA: In my country, truth is often difficult to find, so we
spend much time insisting on it. Unhappily, we often have
different truths in our heads, so we fight. But it is very
exciting that you say you love me, or that you want to love
me, and I'll try to believe that there's some truth in that.

HAROLD: Right. Since we're what my rougher friends call
letting it all hang out, I shall now explain something about
truth, and about me, and about the English, which might
provide an interesting topic for discussion.

JUNE: Go and get the stick.

HAROLD: We have special traditions in England, which is
why we don't talk too seriously about politics, or money or
religion or sex, which anyway we don't understand, despite
the television, though rather surprisingly sex has turned
up this evening because you two seem to be keen on one
another, but not, I hope, so keen as to spoil supper. What
our traditions do allow us to do is talk about our unhappy
childhoods, so here's what we might call my 'stuff', as my
reading has taught me to call it.

JUNE: Please don't indulge yourself, Harold.

HAROLD: I'd like to mention my earliest experience with
what we call, those of us who have read certain books, a

transitional object. Mine, apparently, was a piece of silk from my mother's wedding dress from which I was inseparable from the moment I was weaned, though I have no recollection of it. One day, it seems a man called Uncle Thomas came and took it from me, wiped his nose on it and threw it in the waste paper basket.

(*TONY and TANIA are now kissing, just their lips together rather than a held embrace.*)

JUNE: Tony! Stop it!

HAROLD: You could've waited.

TONY: It was lovely, but not quite complete.

TANIA: A kiss through the barbed wire.

JUNE: It was very hurtful.

HAROLD: For heaven's sake! A man chooses three people – two especially – to expose his innermost bits to, and while he's doing it, they snog each other so that he might as well be exposing himself to a bunch of thistles. And then to cap it all they say the snog wasn't worth it.

JUNE: Harold, this is grown-ups' time.

HAROLD: How was that for destroying someone's sense of identity? For putting the carnal above the spiritual with a capital C. For shitting on someone from a great height with a capital – capital –

TONY: Let's try again.

TANIA: Not yet. This isn't an evening about passion.

JUNE: Isn't it?

TONY: Then what is it about?

TANIA: Peace and understanding and things of that kind.

HAROLD: And culture.

TONY: Why are you so hung up on culture?

HAROLD: You've not tried living without it.

TONY: I do very well without it. I sell rat poison for thirty grand a year and rising, and culture doesn't give you that.

TANIA: There must be more to you than thirty thousand pounds.

TONY: It means you don't have to visit the turkeys at the bottom of the garden.

TANIA: And you can kiss anyone from Eastern Europe that you fancy.

TONY: I've just told you my feelings about that.

TANIA: And in my eyes that was culture.

HAROLD: No it wasn't! Culture is these pictures and long words with special meanings. He's what they call a philistine – philistine?

JUNE: They were people in the Bible who had six fingers.

HAROLD: There, you see? Cultured people know things. Six fingers?

JUNE: Goliath had six fingers.

HAROLD: I thought he had a stone in his forehead.

(*MATHEW enters.*)

MATHEW: All right, Harold, you can go now.

HAROLD: What?

MATHEW: I thought you wanted the toilet.

HAROLD: You're all playing the Great Game aren't you!! You've decided to make me the runt, haven't you! I came here to relish sophisticated society, and all I've got so far is –

JUNE: Go and find the walking stick before he falls down.

MATHEW: I'm taking off my socks.

JUNE: You'll catch your death, your circulation's packing up.

MATHEW: Don't exaggerate.

JUNE: You'll get gangrene. Tell him.

TANIA: Why do you say these things?

JUNE: Because he's my uncle and not your sugar daddy.

TANIA: Don't you suggest that I'm –

JUNE: You're a little golddigger, here to get whatever you can. The place is flooded with the likes of you.

TANIA: I'm not a golddigger!

(*The two women have closed on each other and are quickly separated by TONY and MATHEW.*)

TONY: Tania!

MATHEW: Stop it! Stop it!

HAROLD: June, go and find the walking stick.

JUNE: Who are you talking to?

HAROLD: I'm sorry but I had to speak. Let's go and find the stick together. You want to look nice after all.

JUNE: I am nice.

HAROLD: Yes.

JUNE: I'm very nice.

HAROLD: Yes

JUNE: Niceness is the quality I cultivate most of all.

HAROLD: Yes.

JUNE: Stop saying that! I didn't start it! (*They are off.*)

MATHEW: What's happened to my party?

TANIA: I'm so sorry. That was the last thing I wanted.

TONY: It's all right.

TANIA: I'll take your socks.

MATHEW: Thank you. You're still very beautiful, especially on a late summer evening.

TANIA: I'm very beautiful all the time. It's a bugger.

MATHEW: (*Wiggling his toes in the grass.*) Oh, that's good. I hope June didn't leave any thorns about after the rose bush thing. (*He looks at the other two.*) Not much different from this morning, is it. Each of you wanting me to leave.

TONY: I'd like to leave myself, but I want to be with her.

MATHEW: I'd like you to leave so that I can be with her.

TANIA: I'm hoping nobody will leave and everything will be lovely.

MATHEW: A truly Macedonian hope.

TANIA: A Western hope for Macedonia. A United Nations hope. Everyone in harmony, and no inflamed desires.

TONY: My feelings are better than inflamed desires.

MATHEW: (*With some delight.*) Mine aren't. (*Wriggles toes.*) And their inflammation is wonderful. Let's not pretend things aren't here that are. I am, though, an academic, and there are times when reason breaks out, even among us, so I know I'm grisly, probably older than her father, and though everything is possible, some things are also unlikely. How are your feelings?

TANIA: Mostly that I'm a vulnerable girl in a foreign country. I don't have the signals that would help me understand the depth of people's emotions.

TONY: It feels dangerous to move.

(*After a moment MATHEW walks forward towards TANIA. TONY also walks forward and intervenes.*)

No.

TANIA: (*To TONY.*) Don't touch him.

MATHEW: I was only playing.

TANIA: You were trying to separate us.

MATHEW: Yes. No! Restraint, restraint, let us all be restrained, and not do the things we want! Selfish desires must evaporate, out of the window with them all. Yes, beloved Tania, I will not long for your soft centre, your delicate lips, your skin, your hair – your drenching love. I will be restrained, for peace and understanding matter more than anything. Though what understanding is, God knows. Better than love, probably, but not a lot of fun. Not lively, not – oh God, you are edibly attractive, but I will not want to swallow you, or roll on the grass with you, feel you close – I will not want anything of you that I do actually want like hell. Peace! Break out in my heart and also my loins! Come on, peace!

TONY: It's a bit embarrassing.

MATHEW: Why?

TONY: Can't you control yourself.

MATHEW: Why me and not you?

TONY: Because I have a future.

(*JUNE enters with HAROLD and walking stick.*)

JUNE: It's just like the W.I. marmalade. It hasn't gone yet, though I've pushed it all afternoon, and now I'm stuck with it. Immigrants. (*Stick to MATHEW.*) Here, take this and admit your age.

MATHEW: I hate you, June.

TANIA: Calm down, Mathew.

MATHEW: I hate her from the depths of my soul, but I shan't upset her.

JUNE: (*Offering stick.*) Take it you crumbling bag of bones, you need it.

(*MATHEW seizes it and swings it over his head.*)

MATHEW: I am as young and virile as I ever was!

TANIA: (*Shrieks.*)

TONY: Stop!

HAROLD: Oh! Oh!

JUNE: Help!

MATHEW: I'm only posing. (*Lowers stick, returns to normal.*)

TANIA: Good boy. Well done.

JUNE: Oh, get back to your own country, why don't you? And here, take these with you.

(*She thrusts the picture at TANIA.*)

MATHEW: Did you meddle with my cooking out there?

HAROLD: No, she didn't.

MATHEW: I'll bet she did. She always meddles, exactly like
her mother. (*He goes out.*)

JUNE: (*To TANIA.*) I'm not a racist, you know. I'm just British.

MATHEW: (*Off.*) You've turned it up to Gas Mark 7.

JUNE: We'd be here all night, otherwise.

MATHEW: (*Off.*) It should be Gas Mark 4.

HAROLD: I never saw you.

JUNE: You're blind. Where are you going?

TANIA: To help him.

JUNE: And to fiddle with his trousers, I'll bet.

TONY: Anybody fiddles with people's trousers –

JUNE: You stay there. And Harold keep your distance. (*As she
follows TANIA.*) Keep away from that gas stove, Tania. (*Bobs
back to speak to HAROLD.*) I can see you from the kitchen,
just remember, Harold, and he's mine.

MATHEW: (*Off.*) Clear off, June.

JUNE: (*Off.*) I'm coming to watch.

MATHEW: (*Off.*) There'll only be cooking to see.

TONY: I'd better get in there myself. (*Moves.*)

HAROLD: Don't you trust your Macedonian?

TONY: (*Halts.*) P'raps I'd better.

HAROLD: The thing is, it'd be quite nice to like you, Tony.
Even though you're not sympathetic.

TONY: (*Wary.*) What exactly do you mean?

JUNE: (*Off.*) I can see you.

(*HAROLD nods his head to draw TONY out of JUNE's
assumed eyeline, and moves away a bit himself.*)

TONY: (*Both men drop their voices.*) What is it?

HAROLD: You pity me, don't you.

TONY: I don't. You annoy me.

HAROLD: I made you pity me. I'm good at that, everyone
says so.

TONY: I think I'll go to the kitchen.

HAROLD: You don't understand. There's a divinity that
shapes our ends, rough hew –

TONY: I don't believe in the great game so –

HAROLD: It's there whether you believe in it or not.
You're entangled.

JUNE: (*Re-entering.*) Stay where I can see you.

TANIA: (*Off.*) Oh Mathew.

JUNE: What's that?

TANIA: (*Off.*) Nothing.

JUNE: (*Returning to off.*) Take your feet off her ankles.

TONY: What?

HAROLD: He's just being playful. The thing really is that I don't know anything about anything. I don't know enough to pity people who really suffer. I mean – suffer. I don't suffer. I kind of dip under. To be honest, I don't like standing up straight at all. I don't really occupy all my space. (*Tries.*) Can't do it, you see. June's uncle noticed. I'm always being asked if I want to go to the toilet, and I'm always saying 'No, it's just the way I stand.'

TONY: Where's this leading?

HAROLD: It annoys you?

TONY: I'd quite like to know what you mean, but Tania's in there and –

HAROLD: It's my preoccupation with being, or not managing to be, what you might call placed. I'd like to spend a lot of time floating in a very specific and comfortable area, preferably in the middle classes.

TONY: I have to go and see Tania.

HAROLD: Tony, I don't even know where Macedonia is, let alone what's happening there.

TONY: I don't think many people do.

HAROLD: But you – you even know how to use the dialect you were born with and not sink back into the mire.

TONY: For God's sake, Harold, what's wrong with you? Are you gay or aren't you? Interested in the arts or aren't you? Middle class, working class –

HAROLD: I've no idea! And if I try to answer those intriguing questions, I am deafened by an explosion of conflicting voices.

JUNE: (*Off.*) Where've you gone?

TONY: It's all right.

JUNE: (*Off.*) I've got to stay, because he's showing her how to use an egg whisk.

TONY: Look. Just try to be one thing or another, okay?

HAROLD: What d'you mean?

TONY: Well, sexually for a start.

HAROLD: Are you suggesting something?

TONY: Oh, for goodness' sake –

(*HAROLD produces the stick sharply, to prevent TONY moving away.*)

HAROLD: I'm not pathetic, I'm not dangerous, and I'm not homosexual. I'm not sexual at all. But I do at this moment have the chance of talking to someone who is wonderfully ordinary and doesn't mind it. Tell me how you do it.

TONY: If you want help with life, I believe the going rate is about thirty-five quid an hour.

HAROLD: My therapy was on the NHS.

TONY: You've had some?

HAROLD: I want to be like you, a normal, not unpleasant man, flung my way by the Great Player.

TONY: I think I'll get where June can see me

HAROLD: No.

TONY: Yes.

HAROLD: No.

(*HAROLD tries to prevent TONY from moving several times. TONY dodges. HAROLD pauses. He emits a Japanese squawk, and jumps in the air still watching TONY.*)

HAROLD: I've had assertiveness training.

(*TONY grabs the stick and quite easily wrestles it from him.*)

HAROLD: There. Beaten. What a relief.

TONY: You lost on purpose, and you sighed. D'you always sigh?

HAROLD: Some of us are born to surrender. Take me.

TONY: (*Horrified.*) What?

HAROLD: As your assistant.

TONY: I couldn't. There's application forms, interviews, assessment.

HAROLD: Then assess me.

TONY: No. I can't, it has to be someone higher up.

HAROLD: Can you introduce me to them?

TONY: No.

HAROLD: Why not? It's written in the stars, Tony, my future will be changed by meeting you. Riches selling rat poison, women falling at my feet, classical music, modern art –

TONY: It's not like that.

HAROLD: It is, I read the Daily Mail. I know I'm missing something, just having a relationship with a bus.

TONY: Sit down and have a crisp.

HAROLD: And I want this evening on the patio because I've never had anything like it in my life. Don't spoil it any more, kissing and arguing.

TONY: I'll try.

HAROLD: We could be a winning team in rat poison, couldn't we?

TONY: I'm sorry, Harold, but you'll never make a salesman. You're weak, vacillating, ignorant, and you retreat all the time into failure. To put it as clearly as I can, you're useless.

HAROLD: I said I didn't like you. And I should remind you that the Great Player never makes a mistake. He's brought me here to change my life.

JUNE: (*Off.*) I saw that!

MATHEW: (*Off.*) You didn't.

TANIA: (*Off.*) There wasn't anything to see.

JUNE: (*Off.*) Tony! (*Enters.*) Tony, I regret to tell you my uncle has just handled Tania and she hasn't minded.

TANIA: (*Entering.*) He was simply looking for a cheese grater.

JUNE: I know a grope when I see one.

TANIA: And seeing must be all you've had for years.

JUNE: I'm groped, young lady, more than you can possibly imagine.

HAROLD: Are you ?

JUNE: Yes, and proud of it.

TONY: Let's go.

TANIA: She's the sort of woman who has bones where other women have breasts.

JUNE: I have breasts, Tania, and men have rested on them.

TANIA: They must have slept very badly, then.

JUNE: Ooh, take care, young lady, just take care.

TANIA: You're a peasant.

JUNE: At least my toilet facilities are clean and British poultry leads a healthy life.

TANIA: But not British sheep and cows.

JUNE: And peasant is not an English word because we don't have any.

TANIA: You killed them all?

TONY: Come on.

HAROLD: No!

JUNE: It's you who does the killing.

TANIA: And you who does the bombing, and you don't care who gets hit so long as they're poor!

JUNE: Get out, you scrawny bitch, and leave us to get what warmth we can.

TANIA: Oh, I see. Tell us what happened to Mr Johnson.

JUNE: He died a happy man.

TONY: For Christ's sake, let's get out of here.

TANIA: I won't be thrown out of anywhere, Tony.

TONY: This place is a lunatic asylum.

JUNE: Asylum, yes, well that's not my fault.

TANIA: I'm not going, I am not going.

TONY: What did you let him do?

TANIA: Let?

TONY: Yes.

> (*TANIA slaps his face. HAROLD laughs.*)

JUNE: What's up with you.

HAROLD: Nothing. It's the Great Player having his little game on my behalf. I told you, Tony, I was right

TONY: It was me being jealous. You spend more time with Mathew than with me, and I'm angry.

TANIA: He isn't jealous. He's a gentleman.

TONY: A gentleman –

HAROLD: (*With stick.*) Now everyone stay calm so we can have an intellectual conversation. Everybody eat a crisp, come on. (*He hands crisps round. A short tense silence.*)

TONY: It's stupid. I could be in the pub with my friends.

TANIA: Then go.

TONY: I love you. It's torture

HAROLD: You're probably needy. Would you like to share it with us?

TONY: I'm in bloody love, that's all.

TANIA: Don't swear.

TONY: I'll swear if I like.

JUNE: Personally, I don't like eating with a foreigner because you have to explain so much and speak slowly.

TONY: Look, why are we staying?

TANIA: We've been invited for dinner.

HAROLD: And we're saying things.

JUNE: She's upset Uncle Mathew, too, you know, harping on about Hetty.

TANIA: He's quite at ease with that.

JUNE: What do you know about it? You weren't here when it happened. It was awful, yes, awful. Obviously. He didn't say it was awful, but it obviously was. It had to be, her leaving him after all that time, going off with some flash middle-European you couldn't trust for a second, I imagine. Well, obviously you couldn't, running off with his wife. He had no right to do that, did he. Uncle Mathew's heart is broken, properly and completely broken, and it's obvious. To me anyway.

TANIA: What about yours?

JUNE: Mine's quite all right. Isn't it, Tony.

TONY: I don't give a shit for yours.

HAROLD: That'll do.

TANIA: Did Mr Johnson really die, or did he leave?

JUNE: To me he's dead. Nothing's ever quite what we wanted when we started, is it. Obviously. We all feel that, don't we. Don't we? But that's not heart break, like losing your wife to a lawyer on the Danube Bend. It's just not – very satisfactory. At times. You know? Things get, well – disappointing, don't they. Well, they do.

TANIA: Is he still with you?

JUNE: I'm not mentioning him again. D'you have to eat those things? I can't hear myself think.

TONY: I'm boiling inside, just boiling.

HAROLD: Go and stand on the grass, then. It'll bring you into balance.

TONY: I'm speechless at the things you say. I've never heard anything like them.

TANIA: Your candles are nice, Harold.

HAROLD: Thank you. Tony lit them because my matches were damp.

TONY: They came from your pocket.

HAROLD: Some of us sweat a lot.

TANIA: I don't think I want these pictures.

TONY: Get rid of them then. I don't care.

TANIA: Perhaps they could go back to Help the Aged.

HAROLD: Thank you. June?

JUNE: (*With difficulty.*) Thank you.

(*Silence. Enter MATHEW.*)

MATHEW: Oh, what a pretty picture. Have you tried taking your shoes off?

TONY: So I can stroke a girl's calves?

MATHEW: It's lovely. (*To TANIA.*) Isn't it?

TONY: It's disgusting.

MATHEW: No, it's lovely. And you're still here, Harold.

HAROLD: Yes.

MATHEW: Your bus must be blocking up the streets quite badly.

HAROLD: I haven't got a bus.

MATHEW: Changed your job?

HAROLD: Actually –

TONY: No, he hasn't.

MATHEW: Oh? The meal will be a little while, so what are we talking about?

(*Silence.*)

Well I'm going to feel the grass between my toes. (*He comes near TONY and does this. Sings quietly.*) T'was all through my own jealousy, pom pom, pom pom. Dada da da da –

TONY: Don't try to work me up.

MATHEW: (*To audience.*) I think Jack Buchanan used to sing it. Or was it –

TONY: Just be quiet.

MATHEW: Actually, there's rather a lot of peace about the place. Like in a grave yard.

JUNE: Here's your stick.

MATHEW: I don't want my stick.

JUNE: You can bang the table with it.

MATHEW: (*He takes it. Then to TANIA.*) I found the cheese grater.

TANIA: Mathew, be good.

MATHEW: Shall we go and search for a sauce boat?

(*TANIA can't help giggling.*)

TONY: I don't know how you have the face to come in here and stir things up, considering what you –

MATHEW: It was only a little cheese grater. It could've been a great big fish kettle, and we'd've had to go into the pantry for that. This is my home, you know, to do as I like in.

HAROLD: Let's discuss the happy accident that brought us all together, a fortuitous group of like-minded people, on this truly lovely evening.

JUNE: I've warned you, Harold, you don't have ideas.

HAROLD: But I do. We meet people on life's journey, and we know them for a while, and then, as ships that pass in the night –

MATHEW: We aren't on a journey. We're on a planet. The metaphor is one of stasis, not movement.

HAROLD: Well, I think –

TONY: The happy accident was my meeting Tania. The rest has been torment. I'd like to thump you one, Mathew.

MATHEW: Have a go, then. Here's the stick.

TONY: You're too old.

MATHEW: I am not. Hit me, go on. On my own lawn.

TANIA: Mathew, this is not peaceful.

MATHEW: Goodness, you sounded like a wife.

TONY: Tell us about that. What was your wife like?

MATHEW: I might thump you, you know that?

HAROLD: Let's talk about being on a planet. Come on, it's interesting.

JUNE: We aren't going to have a conversation just because you like it.

MATHEW: Being on a planet is having food or not having food, and we've rummaged over the problem for centuries and got nowhere. Talk about something else, if you have to.

HAROLD: Art.

MATHEW: No.

TONY: Economics.

MATHEW: No.

JUNE: That's why Hetty left you. You'd come home after a day's work and she'd say 'How was it today at the university?' and you'd say 'Don't talk about that,' and so she'd try three or four more subjects and then give up. It's all your fault.

MATHEW: You don't know anything about me and Hetty. D'you know what I said every day when she woke up and kissed me? Or the way I used to push my face around at shaving time to make her laugh? Or what was the name of the lover I had all those years ago before she left me?

JUNE: You never had a lover, you couldn't.

TANIA: Her name was Hermione.

JUNE: He never knew any Hermione.

MATHEW: We don't know anything about each other, ever. It's wonderful.

JUNE: That's not true.

TANIA: It is true.

HAROLD: It could be true

TONY: I know you're a dirty old man.

MATHEW: Yes. I've just discovered that and it's wonderful.

HAROLD: I think it's time for me to talk about the Great Game.

TONY: Oh God, no. Let's have dinner so we can push off.

JUNE: We lose endless customers at Help the Aged through the Great Game.

HAROLD: The Great Game is very comforting and we are all part of it.

MATHEW: Harold, you're a fool, you know that?

HAROLD: Why does everyone say that to me?

MATHEW: Because it's true.

HAROLD: No it's not. It's just that people keep challenging me, don't they, Tony.

TONY: I'd quite like to know why I've fallen so obsessively in love with Tania, yet have to struggle to get near her.

TANIA: You're a young stag and have to be kept at bay.

MATHEW: She fits with your landscape, your bits of the planet, the rooms you made in your head ever since you were a baby, but you don't quite fit hers, and that's that topic finished with, let's try another.

HAROLD: I think they were meant.

TONY: Why did you love Hetty? (*No reply.*) Come on, you fancy Tania because she's sexy, what about Hetty?

JUNE: She was very glamourous.

MATHEW: Not when you got close, and I got very close indeed. I don't know what happens when you get close to people. Everything becomes impossible, like tangled string.

TANIA: Yes.

MATHEW: Yes. We understand, don't we.

TONY: I am going to thump you.

MATHEW: Here. (*Hands him the stick.*) Let's see if you've got it in you.

JUNE: Uncle?

HAROLD: We're here for enlightened talk, and to be honest, you're getting what I might call beyond yourselves.

TONY: Something, of course, you've never done.

HAROLD: Oh you, it's always you! I have people like you on the bus, and not a drop of breeding in them. Not a word of good manners have they ever learnt, and they smoke when they shouldn't, and they won't accept their change, and they hold things up, and they call me darling, and I have eau de nil in my house and I'm proud of it!

TONY: I'm sure.

HAROLD: You haven't laughed at my eau de nil yet, but you would if you had the chance, even though I spoke to you quite intimately.

JUNE: You didn't.

HAROLD: Not like you, you sex starved old baggage.

JUNE: Don't you call me that, who's never felt the itch in your life.

HAROLD: (*Angry.*) Well, I'm sorry, but you're all very nearly disappointing.

TANIA: What's eau de nil?

MATHEW: Blue mud.

TANIA: You have blue mud in your house?

HAROLD: It's paint, and everybody laughs at it and calls it sludge. Even my house reflects my personality.

MATHEW: Why do you torture yourself with failure?

HAROLD: Because I live here inside this flesh, and I want to do something so someone says, 'Well done, Harold. Eau de nil is lovely in your through room with the RSJ.'

TANIA: Is this self-pity?

HAROLD: It's a party. And I may have to cry.

JUNE: You see what independent thinking leads to.

HAROLD: Shut up. (*Takes out hanky.*)

TONY: That came from your pocket. Is it wet?

TANIA: Tony, you say terrible things.

TONY: I'm not going to stand here feeling what I feel for you and not doing anything about it. I'm going to kiss you as you've never been kissed, and make you throb until you drop.

MATHEW: That's rape. I'm going to kiss her with the silken lips of age.

TANIA: I don't want to be kissed at all.

TONY: You're going to be kissed.

MATHEW: By me.

(*Both men are approaching her. TONY still has the stick.*)

TONY: Get off.

MATHEW: You young thug.

TANIA: Get them away!

(*The men are now jostling, and virtually wrestling with each other to be nearest to TANIA. HAROLD pulls at MATHEW and JUNE at TONY, separating them and getting them away from the girl.*)

JUNE: There's me, Tony, there's me.

TONY: I don't want you.

MATHEW: She always had rubber lips as a child, like kissing a tennis ball.

HAROLD: Was there incest?

MATHEW: Don't be stupid.

HAROLD: (*Angry.*) Stop calling me that! Stand still and be peaceful! There! (*He lets go of MATHEW and fumes in front of him.*)

MATHEW: How can anyone stand still with a delicious girl emanating at him from three feet away.

JUNE: (*Still hanging onto TONY.*) That's another reason why she left him, unanswered questions. She'd say 'Have you had a good day' and he'd answer 'What's the meaning of life?' and then say nothing.

MATHEW: You've got the dithers.

JUNE: I haven't. He asked questions all her life to which he offered no answer at all. 'What is the meaning of life?' 'Is there a God?' 'What is a work of art?' 'Why did we fight the second world war?' 'Who won it?' 'What is happiness?' Dry as dust!

MATHEW: Better than rubber lips. Now, go on Tony. Hit me! (*TONY gets free from JUNE and faces him with the stick.*

He takes a swipe or two, but MATHEW dodges.)

HAROLD: This isn't culture. I know this isn't culture.

MATHEW: It's fun though.

HAROLD: No it's not.

(*MATHEW is enjoying his agility. TONY gets quite fierce. But –*)

MATHEW: Ouch ! (*He suddenly limps.*) One of your thorns, June.

JUNE: Hit him, Tony, hit while he's wounded.

TONY: I can't.

JUNE: Go on.

TANIA: No.

TONY: I can't!

MATHEW: Coward. The revenge of the rose tree. (*He grabs half-standard and tugs at it intending to use it as a weapon.*) You won't be able to dodge this. Ow! Ow! (*He has caught his hands or his head on some part of the rose and is pain.*) I'm bleeding like Jesus, hands and feet. Thorns, thorns –

TANIA: You stupid man. This was supposed to be a peaceful evening. (*She takes HAROLD's hanky to bind MATHEW's hand.*)

MATHEW: You were too attractive.

TANIA: It's not my fault.

TONY: Don't touch him.

JUNE: Slut. I wouldn't be surprised if she doesn't rent a baby from her friends to hawk around the tube.

TANIA: (*Angry.*) I have no need of money. My father was able to send me to England because he's a respected engineer who works for a large American company. He has a life style in excess of anything here, and probably more than you, June, could ever afford. His company paid for me to escape the prospect of civil war, and I have a draft at Lloyds Bank that will keep me in comfort for at least a year.

JUNE: Oh, well – that does make quite a difference, doesn't it. I'm sure your very welcome to have dinner with my uncle.

TANIA: I am not proud of this money. It is in American dollars. There is oil and gas in Russia, under the Caspian Sea, and The West, whatever that means, wants to buy it, and the Russians, whoever they are, want to sell it, so it's to be brought across the Black Sea in tanks to Burgas in Bulgaria, piped through our mountains, across Macedonia, into Albania and out onto the Adriatic coast at Vlore. My father is part of that. And the Albanian rebels in Kosovo want to fight my country for nationalistic reasons, to be big and proud, and also to have some control over the pipe, while the Albanians in my country want to stay as they are and profit from the pipe, as do the Albanians in Albania. The Americans don't want to fight the Albanian nationalists in Kosovo, because they saved them from the wild Serbs, but now as part of the UN force, and as interested parties in the pipelines, they may have to, and that makes the Albanians in my country angry and they want to seize the pipe lines for themselves. My father sent me away to escape all this stupidity. He could afford to. He earns money from it. He disturbs the peace, destroys the environment, hampers research into alternative energy, and you, you miserable little woman, are now pleased to greet me because it means that I've got cash, and don't need your help. You stink.

JUNE: There's no pleasing her, is there.

HAROLD: (*To TONY.*) Where is Albania?

TONY: Down the sea from Venice and turn left. (*To TANIA.*) What are you telling us, exactly.

TANIA: That I'm caught up in the planet's mess, and I don't want to be. My father hoped that here there'd be a better place. (*Looking at the paintings.*) Like this.

MATHEW: You tried to tell me all about it in the boat.

TANIA: And you ignored it.

MATHEW: What can I do about it? I'm a single man on a pension. What can any of us do about it? For Christ's sake, I want to be on my patio with my friends. What's wrong with that?

TANIA: It's simply not enough. But you'll never realise until you lose your patio, and your friends, and everything turns upside down.

(*TONY's mobile rings.*)

MATHEW: Oh, his mobile phone. Can't we ever be free?

TONY: (*Answering it.*) Yes? Oh. Oh, hello Nige. Yes, well I got a bit held up. No, not the squirrels. The birds? Yes, well, it's quite a story. Yes. (*Feeble laugh.*) Where are you?

With the lads in the Fox and Firkin. Yes well, I might join you all later but don't hang around. Yes, it would be good to see them, too. Yes. Speak to you soon. (*Switches off. A sheepish grin.*) Life.

TANIA: Why don't you ring Hetty, Mathew, and see if she's still alive.

MATHEW: I wouldn't know what to say.

HAROLD: You could try hello.

TANIA: There's a dangerous word.

MATHEW: I'd only make some joke about goulash again, and she'd hang up.

TANIA: Well, in that case I think I'll go back to St John's Wood, and perhaps home. Like Harold, like June, I'm disappointed.

TONY: I'll come with you.

TANIA: No. You're all foreigners to me. (*She goes.*)

TONY: (*Calling.*) Tania?

MATHEW: We ruined it.

HAROLD: And we're quite nice people, aren't we?

JUNE: I told you to keep your shoes on, but you wouldn't listen.

TONY: You ludicrous old man. I'm not giving up. (*Moves to go.*)

MATHEW: She won't have you. Wrong bit of planet. (*To audience.*) I will not feel sorry for myself, I will not feel sorry for myself, I will not feel sorry for myself.

HAROLD: Can we have our conversation now?
(*No-one answers.*)

The End.

NICE DOROTHY

a play in twelve scenes

Characters

GORDON
a very old man with a Zimmer frame

MARIE
a very old woman with a Zimmer frame

DOROTHY
Marie's middle-aged daughter

HUGH
Gordon's middle-aged son

HARRIET
a girl in her mid-twenties

BILLIE
her younger flatmate

JUDY
a friend of both, in her mid-twenties

ROBERT
a man in his mid-twenties

TREVOR
his flatmate, the same age

ROY
a middle-aged man in a pub

JIM
a young man in a pub

MILLIE
a woman in her early sixties, with a Hoover

A MAN IN A RAINCOAT

Nice Dorothy was first performed at The Orange Tree Theatre, Richmond, on 13 May 1993, with the following cast:

GORDON/MAN, Peter Wyatt

MARIE/MILLY, Caroline John

DOROTHY, Auriol Smith

HUGH, Frank Moorey

HARRIET, Caroline Gruber

JUDY, Amanda Royle

BILLIE, Janine Wood

ROBERT/JIM, Brian Hickey

TREVOR, Timothy Watson

ROY, David Timson

Director, Sam Walters

Designer, Anne Gruenberg

Assistant Director, Sean Holmes

Painter, Simon Brewster

Scene 1

*Enter two very old people from the opposite sides of the stage. They
are walking with the aid of Zimmer frames along a path headed
for each other. Midway along the path, to one side of it, is a rose
bush. The two old people are called GORDON and MARIE.*

MARIE: Been for a walk?

GORDON: To the shop.

MARIE: Why?

GORDON: Sweeties.

MARIE: I might call for one later,

GORDON: There won't be one later. And you'll have to go
round the corridor because it's going to rain.

MARIE: I'll manage that. My Dorothy's visiting,

GORDON: There won't be any sweeties.

MARIE: All going down Milly's red lane, are they?
(GORDON is convulsed with wheezy laughter.)
Common hussie.

GORDON: The Warden's at County Hall again.

MARIE: She never is.

GORDON: She is.

MARIE: Oh – worries you sick.
(Thunder.)

MARIE: Shit.

GORDON: You won't reach your flat before the rain.

MARIE: I will if you move off the path.

GORDON: I want to reach my flat.

MARIE: We'll crash, Gordon.
*(GORDON is now about to pass the rose bush and MARIE
is approaching him.)*

GORDON: You go to the side.

MARIE: You go to the side.

GORDON: You go.
(Thunder.)

MARIE: I'll catch myself on the prickles. Move.

GORDON: I can't. *(His frame is stuck.)* There's a crevice here,
Marie.

MARIE: (*Approaching him.*) Well, shift out of it.

GORDON: I can't shift out of it,

MARIE: Shift.

GORDON: You shift.

MARIE: I can't. (*She now crashes into him and tries to move herself and him somehow.*) Shift!

GORDON: I can't!

MARIE: I want to be free!
    (*Lightning.*)

GORDON: Christ, we'll fry.

MARIE: Help!

GORDON: Help!

MARIE: Help!

GORDON: These frames'll draw down lightning like flies to cow plops.

MARIE: And the Warden's at County Hall. Help!
    (*Thunder.*)

GORDON: Help!

MARIE: Help!

GORDON: Shift to the side, you sheep-faced old sod.

MARIE: Help!

GORDON: Help!

MARIE: Help!

GORDON: Where's your daughter?

MARIE: Help! (*Pulls herself free and GORDON totters over onto the rose bush.*)

GORDON: Aaah!

MARIE: Right. (*She moves on.*)

GORDON: You devil!
    (*There is another flash.*)

MARIE: Help! Gordon's ruining the roses! Dorothy!

GORDON: Help!
    (*Thunder but retreating.*
    Enter DOROTHY, fifties, and wearing outdoor clothes.)

DOROTHY: Whatever's happening, Mother?

MARIE: We're being silly.

GORDON: I can't get up, Dorothy.

DOROTHY: But it's going to rain.

(*As MARIE is moving forward she is driving DOROTHY
back down the path.*)

GORDON: I know. And I'll be struck by lightning.

MARIE: The rain'll put you out if you catch fire.

DOROTHY: The thunder's passing, Gordon.

MARIE: Aren't you going to help him up?

DOROTHY: You're in the way.

MARIE: You hear that?

GORDON: Can't wait for the lightning to get us and save the
crematorium expenses.

DOROTHY: Oh Gordon! Just get off to your nice flat,
Mother, and I'll come in a minute and have tea and talk
about the Queen. (*She goes round MARIE.*)

MARIE: You're not supposed to go on the grass and Gordon's
got some sweeties for us.

GORDON: I haven't.

MARIE: So don't steal those, 'cos I want one. (*She hobbles off.*)

DOROTHY: Are you all right?

GORDON: Am I buggery.

(*Enter HUGH, wearing an overcoat and much the same
age as DOROTHY.*)

HUGH: What d'you think you're doing, Father?

GORDON: Dying.

HUGH: But it's going to rain.

DOROTHY: I'm not sure which bit to lift, either.

GORDON: Will I break?

DOROTHY: No.

GORDON: How d'you know?

HUGH: People don't.

DOROTHY: They do, as a matter of fact. They break very
easily.

HUGH: Dorothy?

GORDON: Don't say frightening things,

HUGH: Well, I've never broken anyone. Imagine it –
I'm sorry Mr Smith, you just came away in my hands.

DOROTHY: I don't think it's a laughing matter. I'm sure I've
broken people, and I know people have broken me, and
all my life there seem to have been splinters of people all

round the place, bits of me, bits of others. It's a mess, a real mess, life. It's a kind of skip.

GORDON: Help.

DOROTHY: I'm sorry, Gordon. (*She and HUGH begin lifting him.*)

HUGH: I've never thought of you as depressive.

DOROTHY: I'm simply offering an observation about life.

HUGH: It isn't true.

GORDON: (*As they lift him.*) Aaah! There's a thorn in my calf!

DOROTHY: I'm sorry.

GORDON: Is it bleeding?

HUGH: Yes.

DOROTHY: Yes.

GORDON: It'll stain my socks, and Milly's washing the others.

DOROTHY: Milly? You're paying her, I suppose.

HUGH: You're meant to wash your own socks, Father, not give your pension to Milly.

GORDON: Get me on my frame and say no more. I've money enough for sweets. (*GORDON is now upright.*)

HUGH: Now, say thank you to Dorothy.

DOROTHY: It doesn't matter.

HUGH: Say –

DOROTHY/GORDON: No.

GORDON: I'm independent, I don't say thank you. (*He goes on his way.*)

HUGH: (*Quietly.*) They say you're an angel. They'll be meeting real ones soon of course, hahaha.

DOROTHY: I'm a very nice person, that's all.

GORDON: It doesn't make a lot of difference, though.

DOROTHY: If I wasn't nice I wouldn't be here to pick you up.

GORDON: You didn't stop me falling, did you. (*Wheezy laugh.*)

(*DOROTHY starts to tidy the rose bush.*
GORDON leaves the scene.)

HUGH: It's terrible when they're so old you can't hit them.

DOROTHY: Are you still caught in that? Trammelled up in honouring thy father and thy mother? (*Silence.*) You'll

have to get over it before he dies or you'll spend half your
income on psychotherapy when you could be giving it to
Oxfam.

HUGH: Why do people say you're nice?

DOROTHY: Because I am, I truly am. I live according to a
simple set of rules – Look Up, Not Down; Look Out, Not
In; Lend A Hand.

HUGH: Does it help?

DOROTHY: Help? I am utterly pointless, Hugh. You may
search through every novel of suburban life, every play by
Chekhov and you will find no woman quite so pointless as
me; untrained, small private income, charitable instincts,
never touched a man and living in Luton. Help? What
d'you mean, help?

HUGH: Dorothy?

DOROTHY: Yes?

HUGH: Are you breaking?

DOROTHY: Of course I am. We're all always breaking. One
minute we are, one minute we're not. It's how life goes,
smash, together, smash, together, smash, together. I must
go to mother. And then I've a niece in Swiss Cottage I'm
very nice to. She's nice to me because I'm nice to her, and
she sings a lot. I once lent her money to help buy a flat.
Have this. (*She gives him a rose which she broke off the squashed
bush.*)

HUGH: Are you proposing to me?

DOROTHY: What?

HUGH: Trying to stop life breaking?

DOROTHY: What do you know about life? That thing that
goes on all over the planet?

HUGH: Well – I work in insurance.

DOROTHY: Well, you can't insure against life. Of course I'm
not proposing. That would be even more pointless. It's not
going to rain, now, and Hugh, I am nice.

(*They leave for their relations.*)

Scene 2

*A sound of birds singing and perhaps traffic. There is a fence divid-
ing the stage. From one side there will appear the boys, from the
other appear now, as from the French windows of a garden flat,
three girls of about twenty to twenty-five. They are HARRIET,
the oldest, JUDY, the most experienced sexually, and BILLIE, the
most vulnerable. They are singing three parts of a madrigal so that
it sounds rather lopsided but nice. They hold music in their hands.
When there is no other sound, we hear the sound of evening birds.*

JUDY: (*Breaking off.*) Why are we doing this?

HARRIET: Because I want us to, and it's my flat, and I
    cooked dinner. Start again, bar eight. (*She starts afresh but
    BILLIE cries. HARRIET takes her in her arms.*) Aah. Breathe
    slowly, love. That's it.

JUDY: She's not having a baby or anything.
    (*Tears increase.*)
    That was a joke.

BILLIE: I usually like jokes. (*More fervent tears.*)

HARRIET: Yes. So healthy.

JUDY: He'd've left you, even if you'd been pregnant, Billie.

BILLIE: I know!

JUDY: Oh Christ. Let's go indoors.

HARRIET: Why?

JUDY: Men might see us.

HARRIET: Men?

JUDY: Some could come out into that garden.

HARRIET: Some do live in that house if you want them.

BILLIE: She doesn't.

JUDY: I might.

HARRIET: She's always going on about penetration and the
    different shapes and –

BILLIE: Please! Remember my broken heart!

HARRIET: There, there, there.

JUDY: There's something about this flat that makes it impos-
    sible to say fuck.
    (*More tears. A young man, ROBERT, has come into the
    garden in the relaxing clothes of evening.*)

HARRIET: Can we all control ourselves? Hello, Robert.

JUDY: What?

ROBERT: Hullo.

JUDY: A miracle. And isn't it a lovely evening for visiting the neighbours.

BILLIE: Can we sing again?

HARRIET: Yes.

JUDY: No.

BILLIE: Yes.

HARRIET: We asked you here to sing, so sing. (*Thrusts music into her hand.*)

JUDY: (*Disparagingly.*) Madrigals.

(*They start.*

TREVOR, another young man, comes into the garden.)

TREVOR: What is it?

ROBERT: Birds. The spring evenings bring them out.

TREVOR: I don't want to meet them, not tonight.

JUDY: (*Still singing.*) There's two now, Harriet.

(*HARRIET keeps them singing.*)

ROBERT: Doesn't it cheer you up?

TREVOR: They don't look as if they come cheap. But it takes you back a bit. Choir practice. Speech day. (*Laughs.*)

(*The girls peter out.*)

HARRIET: That's all we can do with so few people.

JUDY: If you joined us we could make up the proper numbers.

BILLIE: I don't want to meet them.

ROBERT: Trevor's feeling a bit low, actually.

JUDY: Aaah, I've met Trevor. More than met him, I think. At Rupert's.

TREVOR: Oh, really?

JUDY: So come on over, I'm Judy.

HARRIET: I'm Harriet and it's my flat.

TREVOR: Well.

ROBERT: All right.

(*They go into their own house.*)

JUDY: (*Referring to the boys.*) Food! I'm sure I've meet that Trevor. I'll know by the shape.

BILLIE: Judy!

JUDY: Does he have a degree?

HARRIET: We all have degrees, don't we. That's how we escaped.

(*HARRIET's front door bell goes.*)

JUDY: That was quick.

HARRIET: Wait. It's my nice aunt Dorothy. She's been visiting her mother in a charnel house in Harrow and she rushes down the Jubilee Line each time she does it. You haven't met her yet, Billie. You'll like her. It's almost required. (*She goes out.*)

JUDY: This is no time for aunts.

BILLIE: I love someone so much I don't want to see anyone. I don't want to go anywhere because everything I do is what I've done in my head with him so everything hurts me more and more. Life hurts me more and more. I want to die. (*Tears.*)

JUDY: Aaah. Aaaah. I don't understand you at all, but aaah,

(*Enter HARRIET and DOROTHY.*)

HARRIET: This is my Aunt Dorothy – oh, Billie.

BILLIE: I'm sorry. (*Continues crying.*)

DOROTHY: Shall I go?

HARRIET: No, no. She'll dry out soon.

DOROTHY: (*Over the sobs.*) I've been visiting my old mother which is quite a – are you sure she's going to stop?

BILLIE: I'm mad because I love somebody who doesn't love me.

DOROTHY: Oh dear.

HARRIET: But we cured her with madrigals, so she's just pretending. She's my new flat mate.

JUDY: I'm Judy, I'm promiscuous, and I don't cry.

(*Bell again.*)

(*Leaving.*) And here come some boys: boys, boys, boys, but not enough for all of us.

DOROTHY: (*To BILLIE.*) Keeping busy usually helps. And looking up, not down. And with this lovely garden – they do say green is very soothing.

BILLIE: I know all that.

DOROTHY: That's the strange thing. Everybody knows what to do, and it isn't the slightest use.

(*Enter JUDY and TREVOR and ROBERT.*)

JUDY: Robert and Trevor, lovely lads, both of them.

BILLIE: Take them away.

HARRIET: No, no let's all sing madrigals and calm down.

JUDY: Or have a gin and tonic.

BILLIE: I work in publishing with Harriet and my heart's broken.

TREVOR: Oh bad luck. I know a bit how you feel. I just lost my job.

DOROTHY: Oh dear.

(*He turns to look at her.*)

Oh! Oh! How could a person like you lose their job?
I mean who would want to get rid of you, looking like –
I mean so obviously – who'd do that?

TREVOR: My boss.

DOROTHY: What a stupid and insensitive man. You're sure you lost it, and didn't give it up?

TREVOR: Yes.

DOROTHY: It wasn't a hobby or something.

TREVOR: I worked in the city.

DOROTHY: Well, I can't believe it. You're so – you're so – you're so young and – and I didn't catch your name.

TREVOR: My name's Trevor.

JUDY: I met him at Rupert's.

DOROTHY: It's my favourite name.

TREVOR: And you?

DOROTHY: Dorothy, I – er – I suppose I'm Harriet's aunt.

TREVOR: Harriet?

DOROTHY: Over there.

TREVOR: I've only just moved in to share with Robert.

DOROTHY: Oh? Well, I am her aunt, but I am nice.

TREVOR: Pardon?

DOROTHY: You're – you're – What a pretty shirt. Does it have to be ironed?

TREVOR: No.

DOROTHY: So sensible.

ROBERT: Do your menfolk wear non-iron shirts?

DOROTHY: I'm not a mother. I'm just an aunt. Can someone else speak, please?

HARRIET: Good heavens, Dorothy.

DOROTHY: I've a frog in my throat. When you can't speak you have a frog in your throat. And I can't speak, so it's a frog.

JUDY: It's the frog that's talking, is it?

DOROTHY: No, it's me. The frog stops you – Harriet?

HARRIET: Well, what about your mortgage Trevor, if you've lost your job.

JUDY: Harriet!

HARRIET: If he's lost his job he might've lost his bedroom, too.

TREVOR: I'm trying not to think about it.

DOROTHY: I'm sure you'll get another job. I mean, I'd employ you like anything – I mean – you know.

JUDY: You're talking again.

DOROTHY: Apparently –

JUDY: Have you far to go?

DOROTHY: Only Luton. That is St Pancras, the train. No, I haven't far to go. Where did you say you lived?

TREVOR: Next door.

DOROTHY: How nice. I often call on Harriet.

HARRIET: Gin and tonics, I think.

JUDY: Before the old sheep eat the young wolves. Trevor, are you sure you don't remember that night at Rupert's?

TREVOR: Not exactly,
  (*TREVOR, ROBERT and JUDY go in.*)

HARRIET: (*To DOROTHY.*) Are you all right?

BILLIE: (*To the garden.*) I love you Stephen.

HARRIET: (*To BILLIE.*) Hold my hand, love. (*To DOROTHY.*) Aunt Dorothy?

DOROTHY: It's nothing, absolutely nothing. Well just a sort of rope tugging at my – I don't know where, really. I'll join you in a minute.
  (*Door bell rings.*)

HARRIET: It'll be the lady for the Amnesty envelope. (*Calls.*) You can all contribute.
  (*HARRIET and BILLIE go.*)

DOROTHY: Oh God, across a crowded room at my age.

And at his age. I mean it's ridiculous to feel this monstrous
– this wonderful – Oh heavens what's going to happen?
Nothing. Absolutely nothing. It's just that I'm in love that's
all. (*Horrified.*) In – love.
(*Enter TREVOR.*)

TREVOR: Pardon?

DOROTHY: I – I – I –

TREVOR: D'you want to stay out here?

DOROTHY: I've never, ever kissed anyone.

TREVOR: Are you making a rather obvious kind of hint?

DOROTHY: Yes. How awful.

TREVOR: It's all right,

DOROTHY: It's so naked – oh! – I mean obvious. I'm very
sorry. May I try, though?

TREVOR: If you want.

DOROTHY: Thank you. (*She kisses him.*) Is that it?

TREVOR: Well to start with.

DOROTHY: To start with. Oh, well, I'm afraid I have to go
now. I've spent the day visiting my old mother and it's
been really rather exhausting.

TREVOR: Yes.

DOROTHY: Yes what?

TREVOR: I expect it has.

DOROTHY: And your day, of course. Losing your job and
everything. We will meet again, won't we?

TREVOR: I expect so.

DOROTHY: Good. (*She goes.*) There's a bit of dry rot in that
window frame.

TREVOR: What on earth was that? What was that?
(*Enter ROBERT.*)

ROBERT: The girls are waiting.

TREVOR: I don't want to stay long, Robert. It's all been
rather exhausting.
(*They exit.*)

Scene 3

HUGH is seated at a table with another man, rather younger, beside him. This other man is ROY. There are sounds of a bar. Offstage can be heard the sound of a young man speaking as he approaches. His name is JIM.

JIM: (*Off.*) Excuse me, pardon. Excuse me. Oops. Sorry mate, you're wearing a mac, anyway. (*He backs on. He is about thirty and is carrying three pints of beer. He brings these to the table.*) It's so hot in there. So cheers, anyway, Hugh. I suppose at your age it's all grassy uplands.

HUGH: I wish my father would die.

JIM: Oh come on. We're all fathers, Hugh.

HUGH: Not me. I'm just a son, that's all and I wish my father would die.

JIM: I hope my son never says that.

ROY: They all do, Jim, they all do.

HUGH: I love him of course –

JIM: That's something.

HUGH: But I want him dead.

JIM: Ah well, It's a question of getting the thoughts to fit the feelings, or the feelings to fit the thoughts. I'm always saying that to the kiddies. If you can feel what you think, or think what you feel, then – you know. Anyway, that's what I say.

ROY: At bed time?

JIM: Before reading to them. Cheers.

HUGH: I dare say Hitler felt what he thought and thought what he felt.

JIM: It's a question of thinking and feeling the right things, isn't?
(*Bar sounds have faded away.*)

HUGH: Well I love my father, and I wish he was dead; and I bloody well want a bit of life.

JIM: I thought it was our generation that swore, not yours.

ROY: I had a granny used to say 'Shit and fall back in it, you little sods'.

JIM: A granny said that?

ROY: They know about life, you know, the nans. The nineteen-thirties.

HUGH: I'm sick of the nineteen-thirties. No one remembers the nineteen-thirties except my father.

ROY: When were you born, then?

HUGH: Between the slump and Munich.

ROY: I was Hiroshima.

JIM: I was the Beatles.

HUGH: Vietnam.

JIM: Like I say, it depends how you look at it.

HUGH: And I wouldn't mind marrying.

ROY/JIM: What?

HUGH: They say you can be quite happy, married.

JIM: Yes.

ROY: Well, naturally, yes, you can, yes. At times you can be very happy. There's always someone else you can blame when you're married.

JIM: Have you got your eye on someone?

HUGH: Yes.

JIM: Is Cupid shooting her darts, eh?

HUGH: His.

JIM: What?

HUGH: Cupid was a boy.

JIM: (*Shocked.*) Oh.

ROY: Does your father disapprove?

HUGH: It's nothing to do with him. He's just a ghost, beckoning at me.

JIM: It's not a homosexual thing, is it?

HUGH: What I'm considering, if you can feel and think of it, Jim, is affection, the warmth of one human being caring about another human being. I want to be with someone I don't have to manipulate, someone I don't have to make demands on, a person who understands the small things of my life, the very little things, and whose very little things I can understand back. I don't want Tristan and Isolde. I want a warm bum to snuggle up to and fall asleep beside, not anything – erect.

JIM: Oh! Ha ha.

HUGH: Ha ha? I want to fit like a piece of wood into someone else's jigsaw, I suppose I want to enter the human race. Yes, I've got my eye on someone.

ROY: Who?

HUGH: She's called Dorothy, and she fits the bill very nicely.

JIM: Well – this calls for three shorts, I think. Oh yes, it certainly does. Shorts all round. (*He leaves with empty glasses. HUGH's is not empty and so stays there. As JIM goes the sounds of the bar come up and we hear him as he goes off.*) Excuse me. Excuse – empty-handed this time, haha. Excuse me, barman?

ROY: She fits the bill?

HUGH: I think so.

ROY: You can't do that, Hugh. You can't enter the human race like that, because it isn't a jigsaw.

HUGH: Oh?

ROY: It's more like a wasps' nest. And there's too much of it.

HUGH: Are you being racist?

ROY: There it is, crowding in on you everyday, all over the world, hungry, collapsing, organising itself, destroying itself, arguing, fighting, dying in earthquakes, assassinating people, building things, getting rich, getting poor, squashing itself onto public transport, divorcing, marrying, having kids, believing, not believing, going into supermarkets, starving in millions – it's a mess. There's no warm bums going, there's only thrust and reject. Warm bums are the dreams of romantics.

HUGH: I'm not romantic.

ROY: There's more ways than one of being romantic, and yours is the worst. You want peace, don't you. Well, there isn't any.

(*JIM has returned with three short drinks.*)

Ah, thanks.

JIM: Here's to Hugh, and I've brought the dominoes. Threes and fives?

ROY: Yes.

(*The dominoes are counted out onto the table.*)

HUGH: You didn't mean that.

JIM: What?

ROY: Nothing.

HUGH: Were you speaking from experience? Life on the building site bursting out?

ROY: Double six – that's four. (*Lays out domino and scribbles score on paper.*)

HUGH: Double six and three – fifteen – that's eight. Well?

JIM: (*Unable to play, he taps the table and picks up another domino.*) What were you telling him?

ROY: Not to solve things by using other people.

HUGH: He was saying life is hell.

ROY: (*Putting down a domino.*) No score.

(*HUGH is unable to play, taps and picks up one.*)

JIM: (*Putting down domino.*) Fifteen – that's eight. Well, it isn't?

HUGH: Roy said it is. And marriage too, he says that's hell.

ROY: I didn't.

HUGH: You did.

ROY: No.

HUGH: Yes.

ROY: (*Sweeping dominoes to the floor.*) For fuck's sake! When people tell you things, you keep your bloody mouth shut! Who d'you think you are, God?

HUGH: I merely said –

ROY: Fucking insurance agent. What do you know about hell?

HUGH: I try to avoid it.

ROY: Well, keep to yourself, then, and don't trust anyone. That's the way to do that. I'll be here tomorrow, probably. (*He leaves.*)

HUGH: I only wanted affection.

JIM: From – Roy?

HUGH: Are you happy?

JIM: Yes of course. Well, you have to say so don't you? (*Laughs good-naturedly.*)

HUGH: Absolutely not.

JIM: It was a joke. I am happy.

HUGH: I really love my father, and I can't stand him. And I'm very fond of Dorothy, and I want to marry her. I wonder if any of it's going to work out?

JIM: Well, as I tell the kiddies –

HUGH: Go and put something loud on the video machine. I need some fresh air. (*He leaves.*)

JIM: You haven't drunk your short. (*Bar sounds.*)

Scene 4

A chair in the middle of the space. Sound of a vacuum. Enter MILLY, a woman in her early sixties. She is pushing the vacuum and muttering to herself. She stops and continues very loudly to herself.

MILLY: I'll have that Hugh, I'll have that Hugh, I'll have that Hugh. (*To the audience.*) I'm Milly, another resident in these flats for elderly persons, I talk to myself and this vacuum's very useful if I want to keep what I say secret, which all of us do from time to time, being private individuals. I'm useful here because I'm very helpful. The warden, of course, is the most helpful of all, but she's so often at County Hall, where (*Whispering confidentially to audience.*) they talk of selling things off. Care in The Community, Age With Dignity. (*Stops whispering.*) So I'm what is called an Enabler. (*Dreadful grin.*) I do the little errands, break the little rules that make things irksome, take my little cut occasionally and become indispensable. People tell me things, you see, they always have, I don't know why. When people say 'Milly, you are so good,' I just say, 'No, I'm not good, I'm lucky. I take on people's burdens and I'm lucky.' My husband used to say I'd wear myself out being lucky but I didn't. Wore him out really. (*Laughs.*) No, he was a good man, and I wouldn't like to spoil the memory by marrying again. That's what I tell them, and it hurts them but they understand eventually.

GORDON: (*Off.*) Milly?

MILLY: In you come, Gordon, the door's on the latch like it always is.

(*He enters on his frame and she goes on confidentially.*) Sweet old thing, Gordon, with a son in insurance called Hugh, (*winks.*) doing nicely, unmarried but a bit of a cold fish, though I've had my thoughts, and you've overheard them. (*To GORDON.*) That's it, Gordon. Where's your socks? (*We see the socks hanging out of one trouser pocket.*)

GORDON: In my pocket, soaked in blood from that do in the roses.

MILLY: Aah. Shall I get them out?

GORDON: I suppose so.

MILLY: As you wish. (*She switches on the hoover. She puts her hand in the pocket without socks in it. She rummages about in there. GORDON protests.*)

GORDON: No! No! The other pocket! Ooh! Stop it! Milly!

MILLY: What?

GORDON: The other pocket! Stop!

MILLY: No socks, Gordon.

(*He indicates.*)

MILLY: Oh! This pocket. (*She takes them out. She switches off the hoover.*)

GORDON: You've no right to go messing about.

MILLY: There's usually sweeties in there.

GORDON: I've had them all myself. You, you fiddle with whatever you can find, don't you?

MILLY: I've told you Gordon. I couldn't spoil the memory.

GORDON: But you've cut a hole in my trousers pocket just the same.

MILLY: We're all human. Did you want to talk?

GORDON: Yes. Can I sit? Only my leg'll swell with suppuration from the roses if I don't. (*He gets to the chair.*)

MILLY: Is it about Hugh?

GORDON: He's a good lad.

MILLY: Has he been saying things about the pension book?

GORDON: No.

MILLY: You can have it back, you know. It's only because you said you'd like me to save you trouble.

GORDON: He's lonely. And he's got a lovely house in Cricklewood.

MILLY: Does he bath regularly?

GORDON: Why, does he smell?

MILLY: How should I know? Of all the suggestions! (*Turns on hoover and begins furiously cleaning round the chair.*) Me, sniffing round your son!

GORDON: Milly!

MILLY: It's most unpleasant. Lift your feet up.

GORDON: I can't.

MILLY: I'll have your slippers up the tube if you don't.

GORDON: Stop! Please!

(*She does, and then pulls his Zimmer frame away.*)

MILLY: Now. Do you or do you not want me to marry him?

GORDON: Good God, no. You're too old and bossy.

MILLY: Then what are you saying, misleading me with every word?

GORDON: I'm not saying. I'm asking. Should I suggest Dorothy?

MILLY: No!

GORDON: She's nice and kind and helpful.

MILLY: She's a bag of lavender, no guts, no spirit, and here she wanders in to my flat bold as brass. What are you doing, Miss?

(*DOROTHY appears.*)

DOROTHY: Oh! What a mistake, I am sorry.

MILLY: This is private.

DOROTHY: I was daydreaming, coming to talk to Mother about something.

MILLY: The pension book?

DOROTHY: No, you've beaten me over that.

GORDON: Marriage?

DOROTHY: Well, we mustn't rush things, must we. But I can't keep quiet about it –

MILLY: What?

DOROTHY: I'm in love.

GORDON: With Hugh?

MILLY: Of course not, he's mine.

GORDON: He's not.

MILLY: Well, he's on offer generally. Who is it?

DOROTHY: Nobody you'd know. I must go and talk to Mother. D'you want your frame?

GORDON: I do. All this excitement.

MILLY: Sit down.

GORDON: (*Wriggling.*) I must.

DOROTHY: (*Giving it to him.*) Will you manage in time.

GORDON: Of course I will.

MILLY: That's right, interfere with my conversation! (*As they go.*) You lovesick ninny, what d'you know about it? And remember this place is mine, wandering all over like you have a right! It's mine, and no-one messes with my place because if they do – (*Turning to audience.*) We all have our places, don't we, especially if there's nothing else. And this place is all there is for me, my hole in the corner, and I'm not having it disturbed by randy spinsters. She's no idea! It's us who persevered with our husbands and who know all about that! I'll spoil your chances Miss, you see. If they sell this place, maybe there's things I'll settle to my advantage. I'm mean as hell when I'm bitten, and I've got fourteen pension books! (*She hoovers herself away.*)

Scene 5

The same as the first scene without the rose bush. DOROTHY enters.

DOROTHY: I don't know where to go to meet him. I don't know what to wear to please him. I stand here outside my mother's flat and I can't think of anything but him, in his garden – I never saw him there, of course, but he was in it just before we met – or standing in my niece's sitting room, which is full of rubber plants and classical music, and I wanted him. Oh, how I wanted him.

MARIE: (*Off.*) Dorothy? It's ever so cosy in my little flat.

DOROTHY: (*To the audience.*) It's stuffy, like a burrow. That's all there is ahead of me as I grow older and I want tremendously to kiss him more and more.

(*Enter MARIE on her frame.*)

MARIE: They dug up the broken roses, you see. That was Milly, put them in a pot. Never misses a chance, unlike you.

DOROTHY: Well now, I want to talk to you about that. I've always been very helpful, haven't I?

MARIE: Hah. That nice Dorothy.

DOROTHY: I am nice. People always said so. (*Hand on frame.*) No, stay still.

MARIE: I have to move or I seize up.

DOROTHY: You aren't going to move until you answer me. I need to know that I am nice.

MARIE: Move.

DOROTHY: I'm nice.

MARIE: I can scream, you know.

DOROTHY: I'm nice.

MARIE: Stop it.

DOROTHY: Nice mother, nice. Scream away.

MARIE: All right, you're nice. Nice, nice, nice! Cotton wool! Now move.

(*DOROTHY grasps the frame with both hands at the front.*)

DOROTHY: I won't. You're a terrible old clamp. You grasp things and you never let them go.

MARIE: Help!

DOROTHY: You hang on to what you've got, like me, for instance, and you turn and turn the screw until we howl with being constricted. You're a boa constrictor.

MARIE: Help!

DOROTHY: And what is amazing is that I've remained a thoroughly charming and delightful woman, living on a modest income thanks to Father, topping it up with little jobs and working free for the Samaritans, and I'm a pillar of the community. I'm bloody wonderful, Mother.

MARIE: Help!

GORDON: (*Off.*) What is it?

MARIE: I'm seizing up! Get Milly!

DOROTHY: You're not seizing up.

MARIE: I am. I loved you. I really did.

DOROTHY: I know you bloody did. But tell me that I matter.

MARIE: Of course you matter. All that heaving and shoving and pain, and I wanted a child like anything. I wasn't going to let you go after that.

GORDON: Milly's sweeping.

MARIE: Clots are forming all through me. Jellied blood. She's killing me.

DOROTHY: (*Anguish.*) I'm not. (*She still holds the front of the frame with both hands.*)

MARIE: Oh yes, you are.

DOROTHY: Oh no, I'm not.

MARIE: Oh yes you are.

DOROTHY: Oh no I'm – I could tip you over onto the ground and leave you, you know.

MARIE: There'd be no money. I spent what he didn't leave you from the stores on an annuity, so you'll get nothing.

DOROTHY: Mother, I matter anyway, pain or no pain. I'm lovable.

(*GORDON appears on his frame.*)

GORDON: You're what?

DOROTHY: Lovable. Aren't I?

MARIE: Yes, if you insist.

DOROTHY: I do.

MARIE: Then yes.

(*DOROTHY lets go of the frame.*)

That's better. I can churn everything up now. (*She begins to move.*)

GORDON: She's in love, you know.

MARIE: What?

DOROTHY: I love a man.

MARIE: Oh, that's it. Thank goodness.

DOROTHY: What?

MARIE: You need that, with all those dried up juices making you awkward.

DOROTHY: Don't you call me dried up, you withered old –

MARIE: Get off to your man, go on.

GORDON: I used to love a lot – women, as I recall.

MARIE: I loved your father. I know I did.

GORDON: Where are you going?

MARIE: Round and round.

GORDON: You're not allowed on the grass.

MARIE: Where else is there?

DOROTHY: So you think it's all right to – to –

MARIE: Are you having jiggy-jigs?

DOROTHY: Mother!

GORDON: (*Chortles.*) Jiggy-jigs!

MARIE: Are you asking permission? If you want sex, you have it, at your age

DOROTHY: (*Grasping frame again.*) It's not just sex.

MARIE: Give over.

DOROTHY: It's not just sex.

MARIE: All right!

GORDON: It was just sex with me.

MARIE: Let go.

DOROTHY: Say it and mean it.

MARIE: Help!

GORDON: You'll have Milly out, and us on the grass.

DOROTHY: It's a sort of madness.

GORDON: That's sex.

DOROTHY: All right. (*She lets go.*) But I love him. He's beautiful, and he's about twenty-five.

MARIE/GORDON: Twenty-five?

MARIE: Oh Dorothy.

GORDON: He's after your money.

DOROTHY: I haven't any compared with what they earn these days. I think he loves me.

MARIE: He's after your money. It can't be your body.

(*DOROTHY grabs the frame.*)

All right, all right, he loves you. And I love you too.

GORDON: Can't we go somewhere interesting?

MARIE: We haven't got our hats.

GORDON: I'm off.

MARIE: Don't leave me.

GORDON: Come with me then.

MARIE: When Dorothy comes we have tea and talk about the Queen.

DOROTHY: I'm going to be happy, Mother.

GORDON: I know how you feel. Happened to me in a cinema, once, and I was up before the magistrates in no time.

DOROTHY: But I'm going to be happy because I'm really nice, aren't I Mother.

MARIE: Oh Christ, not again – Yes!

(*Enter HUGH.*)

HUGH: Ah Dorothy. Are you staying a bit or can I give you a lift anywhere?

DOROTHY: Now?

HUGH: I was just calling on father but if you're leaving –

DOROTHY: It's a bit out of your way, but there's this sort of niece I visit from time to time and I thought -

MARIE: Harriet?

DOROTHY: Yes.

MARIE: Bottom end of the family and climbed up. Say hello from me.

HUGH: I'll take you.

(*GORDON has been making his way off stage.*)

GORDON: (*Off.*) Have you come to see me then, Hugh?

HUGH: Yes, but I changed my mind, Dad. Milly'll get what you need. She's got the pension book.

GORDON: She wants to marry you.

HUGH: (*To DOROTHY.*) I'd like to talk to you about that sort of thing, really.

DOROTHY: I've nothing to say, as you well know. Goodbye, Mother.

(*They go.*)

MARIE: Dorothy.

(*DOROTHY turns.*)

Don't make them laugh at you.

HUGH: What does that mean?

DOROTHY: Nothing.

(*HUGH and DOROTHY leave.*)

GORDON: They say they're coming and then they don't.

MARIE: Children always let you down. What's happening in the warden's office? (*She is now nearly offstage.*)

GORDON: After our savings, I should think.

Scene 6

The two gardens again. To the boys' garden enters TREVOR with chairs and table and also DOROTHY and HUGH. Birdsong.

TREVOR: Apparently Harriet doesn't get back till late on Tuesdays, but do wait here.

DOROTHY: Thank you, that's very kind. Unless we're stopping you from –

TREVOR: I'm all too free.

HUGH: The garden's yours?

DOROTHY: This is Hugh, who's given me this lift to see Harriet.

HUGH: And who's waiting to take her home,

DOROTHY: No, he isn't. I said in the car you needn't feel obliged.

HUGH: There's no obligation.

DOROTHY: Then go whenever you want, like now.

TREVOR: (*Leaving.*) I'll get some wine.

HUGH: I have things I want to say to you.

DOROTHY: It'll be ages here and I want to talk to Trevor – Harriet! – talk to Harriet – about all sorts of things, like money, because although she's paid back the capital there's the interest, though in these times it's hard to see –

HUGH: I'll wait in a pub or somewhere.

DOROTHY: I'll take the tube.

HUGH: It's dangerous.

DOROTHY: I'll take the risk as well. Now go.

HUGH: Is something wrong with me?

DOROTHY: Not from a distance.

HUGH: When you gave me this rose –

DOROTHY: It's very faded.

HUGH: I'm not interested in symbols. I'm in insurance and I want to talk properly.

DOROTHY: So do I but not to you. (*Silence.*) And I thought the whole financial market worked on symbols, confidence and things like that.

HUGH: I want to talk about us.

DOROTHY: What County Hall is going to do, you mean, selling off the flats and sending our parents back to live with us.

HUGH: What?

DOROTHY: Well?

HUGH: Good God, I hadn't thought of that.

DOROTHY: I know.

HUGH: Oh, heavens, Father moving out.

DOROTHY: I don't want to talk about it now, because I might run out of steam before Trevor gets back and that's the worst thing.

HUGH: The worst thing is having my father living in my house.

DOROTHY: Look Up, Not Down, Look Out Not In, Lend A Hand. Oh how lovely!

(*TREVOR has entered with a tray and pours three glasses of wine.*)

TREVOR: Robert and I often have a drink out here when we get back from work, except of course I have no work, now.

DOROTHY: Where is Robert? A small one for Hugh, he's leaving.

TREVOR: He's taken Harriet's flat-mate out, the girl with the broken heart.

HUGH: Dorothy was only saying the other day how people broke.

DOROTHY: His father fell in a rose bush. Are you off?

HUGH: It was the rose bush that broke, in fact, and Dorothy saved my father, because she's kind, and now he's going to live with me.

DOROTHY: Oh go, will you, go, go.

HUGH: Why? Oh! You mean – Right.

TREVOR: Are you two –

DOROTHY: No!

HUGH: Are we what?

DOROTHY: We aren't anything except the children of old people. Hugh lives in Cricklewood, and is being courted by a lady called Milly who has made a fortune out of other people's pension books. Now swallow that and go.

HUGH: I hope you know what you're doing because I think you're going off the rails.

DOROTHY: Yes I am.

HUGH: Treat her kindly because she's nice.

DOROTHY: I'm awful!!!!! I'm filthy!!!! I'm wonderful!!!!

HUGH: Is it this way?

TREVOR: Yes.

HUGH: Right.

(*They go out and leave DOROTHY.*)

DOROTHY: (*To the audience.*) I think being alone with the object of your desires – your enormous and overmastering desires – oh! – is the most terrible thing in the world. I feel marvellously trapped and I don't know what's going to give way. The pearly gates must be just like this.

(*TREVOR comes back.*)

TREVOR: You look nervous.

DOROTHY: I'm sorry about that outbreak. No, I'm not nervous, yes, I am, dreadfully, no, I'm not. It's the wine. I'm not used to wine without food.

TREVOR: Nuts.

DOROTHY: What?

TREVOR: There. (*He points to nuts.*)

DOROTHY: Ah! (*She grabs a handful.*)

TREVOR: There's no need to hide behind them.

DOROTHY: No.

TREVOR: We kissed, Dorothy.

DOROTHY: Yes.

TREVOR: What do we do next?

DOROTHY: I don't know. You're the young one, so you're supposed to know what happens.

TREVOR: Not with older people.

DOROTHY: But I have no experience at all. I'd like you to know some things about me first. I live in an ordinary road of ordinary houses, and I smile a lot, which changes the way the house is, especially when I sing. I sing music hall songs – 'Any old iron, any old iron'. Everybody used to know that, once.

TREVOR: A long time ago.

DOROTHY: (*Tartly.*) My father taught it to me. They obviously didn't sing it when I was growing up.

TREVOR: D'you like the past?

DOROTHY: No, it's mouldy. My father's miserable drapery emporium. I live in the future, which smells of the sea. I suppose I mean I live in hope, which is rather forbidden these days. Hope is supposed to stop people making decisions.

TREVOR: Hope's all I've got at the moment.

DOROTHY: Oh, poor you. Well, in these harsh times decision making seems all the rage so everyone discusses what stops people doing it. Those people who say they know how to make decisions tell us what it is all the time – politicians, psychologists, clergymen, people with salaries. People who earn their livings thinking for the rest of us. They say it's hope, sitting around hoping. That's what it is that keeps things in a mess. But for those of us who find decisions just aren't possible, or are very difficult for one reason or another, like starving in a desert, or being shot, or – living in Luton – there is only hope. We hope that there'll be something in our lives that will budge. Budge is a lovely word, don't you think? It leads in the end to the word avalanche.

TREVOR: So shall we kiss again?

DOROTHY: Oh, yes. Avalanche.

TREVOR: Open wide, but not too wide.

(*HARRIET appears in the next-door garden.*)

HARRIET: Hello, Trevor. Oh, Aunt Dorothy. You look like a gold fish.

(*They have been interrupted an inch or so away from each other. They don't move but talk from where they are.*)

DOROTHY: Are you all right dear?

HARRIET: Yes. Shall I come over, or will you come here?

DOROTHY: I should have a bath if I were you.

HARRIET: Would you?

DOROTHY: Yes.

TREVOR: Yes.

HARRIET: Oh.

DOROTHY: See you later, then, to talk about interest repayments and things. You've some dry rot in your window frame.

HARRIET: Have I? All right, then. I'll put on some music.

(*She goes in, pausing to look at the French window as she passes. The lovers don't kiss but turn away to talk.*)

DOROTHY: Do you know a lot about girls?

TREVOR: Well, I've – D'you want to mother me, is that it?

DOROTHY: I want to love you. However, we'd better mention my body. Don't you find it disgusting?

TREVOR: I haven't seen it yet.

DOROTHY: It'll rot before yours.

TREVOR: Perhaps I need it. Perhaps I was weaned too early. Mother never smiled. Love turns out to be so explicable these days. Now we don't die of all those plagues, we all spend time making love and then seem driven to explain why.

DOROTHY: You don't have any plagues?

TREVOR: No. The worst thing about modern love is the way people make it all so very healthy, so that a good fuck is like a plate of muesli.

DOROTHY: Oh –   ah –

TREVOR: I'm sorry,

DOROTHY: No, no, I'll learn the jargon in time. Probably.

TREVOR: People want to make love into a moral imperative. I don't suppose we're moral or immoral, it doesn't enter into it. I just want so much to have you reaching up to me, to feel your whole life close against me, to run my fingers over your sweet lines and know that they've grown over a life time, that I can scarcely find breath for the words. I just long for the touch. Don't you?

DOROTHY: Well, as a matter of fact I'm a bit taken aback, but yes – oh – oh dear – I long for quite a lot of things – you heard me, shouting. Except you haven't any lines, so it's smoothness I long for, but I don't know whether you still have that, or whether you don't, but anyway – It would be staggering to find out.

(*Music comes from next door.*)

TREVOR: There's a lock on the door, so we'll be safe.

HARRIET: (*From just inside her French window.*) I think I will just have a bath, Auntie.

DOROTHY: What a very good idea.

HARRIET: And I have got dry rot. (*She disappears.*)

DOROTHY: (*To TREVOR.*) I've never seen a man without his clothes on, even, let alone – rampant. My father always said 'It's never too late', and oh goodness he was right. I'm shaking in every possible direction. Is the bedroom this way?

(*For the moment MILLY appears with an official-looking MAN.*)

MILLY: If you're the man from Social Services at County Hall, I'd like to say I'm the person who really knows how these flats are run, and I know who's nicely placed to move out into their family's accommodation.

MAN: It's possible we may find that quite useful, though of course the whole matter is still under review.

MILLY: Oh yes? Well, Milly's the name and I'm an enabler. (*Fearful smile.*)

Scene 7

The scene is the two gardens again, it is night time and there is light from the flat belonging to HARRIET. There is also music from this flat. Enter HARRIET. She looks across to the darkened garden on the other side.

HARRIET: (*To the audience.*) I wonder if I ought to put a stop to that? It is such a gift for her, though, rather like an extra bonus on your life insurance. And is one responsible for one's aunt's behaviour, or for that matter her pain? It's very good to feel one is through so much of that oneself. (*The door bell.*)
Coming!
(*Music off.*
There is a knock on the door of the boys' flat.)
JUDY: (*Off.*) Trevor? Trevor?
(*HUGH can be heard speaking offstage on the side of HARRIET's flat.*)
HUGH: (*Off.*) Good evening, I'm very sorry to trouble you, but is your name Harriet, and do you have an Aunt Dorothy?
HARRIET: (*Off.*) Come in.
JUDY: (*Off on the other side.*) Damn, No-one there.
(*HUGH and HARRIET enter from HARRIET's flat.*)
HUGH: That's the garden where they were sitting.
HARRIET: Are you the police?
HUGH: I'm a friend of your aunt's and I left her siting there with a young man several hours ago.
HARRIET: And you're distressed at the thought of her suffering harassment of some kind?
HUGH: I'm jealous.
HARRIET: Oh! Were you –
HUGH: I hoped we'd be affectionate and get married.
HARRIET: Instead of which –
HUGH: At her age all this is unhealthy. And she might take it seriously.
HARRIET: I should think she will.
HUGH: She can't. He's young, he's got a life ahead of him.
HARRIET: He's out of work.

HUGH: We've all got things to do in this world and we can't get bogged down in romantic sex. She needs to settle down and realise that life isn't made up of obsessions.
It's all about hobbies and reading books, and discussing what things mean.

HARRIET: You did that with Dorothy?

HUGH: We'd made a start. My father fell into a rose bush – I told you.

HARRIET: No.

HUGH: I told someone. We must get her out of there.

HARRIET: No, we mustn't.

HUGH: She'll be scarred.

HARRIET: Only for a little while, and all experience is beneficial in the long run. She could be happier for it. (*Bell.*)
Collecting for the Kurds, I expect. We'll carry on in a second. (*Exit.*)

HUGH: (*Calling.*) Suppose she isn't happier? Suppose she's miserable? (*Turning to the empty, darkened garden.*) Dorothy? You could be miserable in there so come out. And you're taking all sort of risks I for one would never insure against. Look, I'm the loyal one, I'm the lonely one, I'm the really nice chap, who's been sitting in the car at the end of the street for hours and hours.
(*Enter from HARRIET's flat JUDY and HARRIET.*)

JUDY: Hello.

HUGH: Hello, I'm a bit disturbed.

HARRIET: Obsessed.

JUDY: Dreadful isn't it. It's like athlete's foot, itchy and you can't let go. I love it. I've got an obsession of my own, that's why I'm here. What's yours?

HUGH: Harriet's Aunt.

JUDY: Oh, funny little Dorothy. Who'd've thought she did that to people?

HARRIET: He's rather carpet slippery about her and he's called Hugh.

JUDY: My obsession has nothing to do with carpet slippers. I can't take my eyes off his belt. He's out at the moment or I'd be scratching away like mad.

HUGH: I've seen you all evening over there, knocking on the door, going away, coming back, knocking on the door, going away, coming back.

JUDY: That's it. His name's Trevor.

HUGH: Trevor?

JUDY: Trevor. (*To HARRIET.*) I've come in the hope of a drink.

HUGH: At this moment, Trevor's got his belt off in respect of Harriet's Aunt.

JUDY: What?

HUGH: Dorothy, passion, flesh. We've missed out.

JUDY: You mean his flesh against hers?

HUGH: Chalk and cheese, really,

JUDY: Tall white cliffs and very mouldy Gorgonzola. Trevor! You're being perverted!

HUGH: Dorothy! She's a lovely woman. Dorothy! You're doing wrong!

JUDY: She's not doing wrong, she's stealing my goods. I've prior claims on that young man. Trevor! I'm going round to pour water on them.

HUGH: You said you can't get in.

JUDY: I'll climb across.

HUGH: These walls are covered with broken glass; keeps the premiums down.

JUDY: Shit. You financial wizards spoil everything.

HARRIET: You've only met him once.

JUDY: Once before and it was grade A. It's she who's only met him once. She's crafty Hugh, you watch her, behaving like a central European savage.

HUGH: Bitch!

JUDY: That's right, you tell her.

HUGH: I adore her, bitch that she is. I want her to keep my life in order.

HARRIET: Will that be very demanding?

HUGH: Yes, it will (*To the pacing JUDY.*). Stand still! I'm sorry. Yes, it takes a lot out of me, keeping myself in order. I have large feelings. Dorothy! Come out! You're only doing this because he's out of work and you feel sorry for him!

JUDY: Is that true?

HUGH: Obviously.

JUDY: I'll get him a job then. Trevor, I'll get you a job!

HARRIET: I thought your own job was at risk.

JUDY: It is, but if I tell him I can get him –

(*Light on in boys' flat.*)

Ah!

(*They gaze across.*

Enter ROBERT and BILLIE.)

JUDY: Oh Robert. You know what's happening in there, I suppose.

ROBERT: No.

HUGH: Sex.

JUDY: Your friend is having sex with an old woman.

HUGH: She's mature, she isn't old.

JUDY: She's old, and she's having horrible experiences.

(*BILLIE cries.*)

Oh God, is she still fantasising?

BILLIE: I want to be in Worcester.

ROBERT: It's been like this all night. I'm here, Billie, and I think you're beautiful.

BILLIE: But you're not him. (*She cries and kisses him and they stay kissing until the end of the scene.*)

JUDY: It's a bordello over there. I've never felt so left out of practical life before. I'm going round. Coming? (*She leaves.*)

HUGH: Yes, I think so.

HARRIET: They won't like it and there may be fighting.

HUGH: I feel like fighting.

HARRIET: No, Hugh, stop. D'you sing madrigals?

HUGH: Madrigals? There's a young ram in there with my lady friend and – madrigals?

HARRIET: As you said when you came, there's a need, as usual, to keep calm, to reach a plateau of content. Only then will you be able to match yourself with my aunt in a suitable and fully fruitful way, which is how life ought to be. Calm. Cool. Unemotional. Unswept by deviating passions. Deeper, richer, and free of peak experiences. Madrigals, in fact.

HUGH: I'm tone deaf.

HARRIET: Then is there somewhere you feel utterly at ease where we can go until this overheated turmoil has abated?

HUGH: Well, sort of.

HARRIET: Then take me there. Perhaps we can feed you back into your own true life, and so into Dorothy's. Hold my hand.

HUGH: That window needs seeing to.

(*She leads him away. He wants to stay. Her light goes out.*)

Scene 8

The light is still on in the boys' garden and ROBERT and BILLIE are still kissing. The kiss breaks.

ROBERT: He's never coming back, you know.

BILLIE: I'm still hoping.

ROBERT: Well, hope is something you shouldn't have. It stops life going on.

BILLIE: Haven't you ever felt the need for hope?

ROBERT: What?

BILLIE: People who haven't felt awful don't know what awful is, Robert, that's why they say that sort of thing about hope.

ROBERT: I'm not being unsympathetic or anything –

BILLIE: You want me to be normal, fruitful, jolly nice to kiss after work.

ROBERT: Didn't you like it?

BILLIE: It was lovely, but I feel unfaithful, and so I feel miserable, and how people feel, is what they are, just as much as what they do, only the people who do things never get around to understanding. (*She cries again.*)

ROBERT: Aah. (*He goes to kiss her. She stops crying for a moment, separates from him before he can do so, stands back, aims and slaps his face.*)

BILLIE: You can't use sex as a handkerchief. (*She cries again.*)

ROBERT: I'm not doing! I absolutely worship the ground you walk on, I feel the air pulsating round you, everything about your proportions is amazing. I want to be part of you

and I don't remember feeling this since I was twelve.
At my prep school. She taught French and wore grey
pleated flannel skirts.

BILLIE: Stephen was in love with his nanny, and he felt so
lonely that he used to cry a lot when we went out together.
I used to tell him what it was like being lonely in a girl's
dorm, and how we used to kiss a lot to overcome it, but he
wasn't very into kissing.

ROBERT: I am.

BILLIE: What happened with your teacher?

ROBERT: I became very good at French. And I've always
loved girls who would look good in grey flannel, which
probably is why I've fallen in love with you.

BILLIE: It's no good.

ROBERT: Yes it is.

BILLIE: I love Stephen.

ROBERT: Bugger Stephen.

BILLIE: He was beautiful.

ROBERT: What did he look like?

BILLIE: It was the way he felt that I remember.

ROBERT: How did he feel?

BILLIE: He kind of came into my veins.

ROBERT: I want to do that.

BILLIE: They're occupied.

ROBERT: By a man you can't remember?

BILLIE: I can remember if I try very hard! And I have a right
to love him, like we all have rights and like we all have to
hope that we can get things, and you're not to say I can't
remember him, because I can! (*She slaps his face again.*)

ROBERT: Stop it!

BILLIE: I can't. I want things to be as they aren't!
(*She howls.*
There is a knocking on the boys' front door.)

JUDY: (*Off.*) Let me in!

ROBERT: Shut up! I love you and come away to Paris for the
weekend.

BILLIE: You don't know what love is. (*Howls on.*)

JUDY: (*Off.*) I don't know who's making that noise, but I want
to be in that garden working on somebody's belt.

ROBERT: Oh, sex! I'm glad I work in tea. (*He exits to open his front door.*)

BILLIE: (*Her sobs reducing to heavy breathing.*) Oh, Oh, Oh – my stomach aches with it all. Where do you put all this feeling?

JUDY: (*Off.*) Well, hammer on the bedroom door.

ROBERT: (*Off.*) No.

(*ROBERT enters bringing JUDY.*)

Now sit down.

(*She does.*

To BILLIE.) Howling the night away again?

BILLIE: Why are you here?

JUDY: Because a beautiful pelvis is being wasted away in that bedroom.

BILLIE: Why should it be more wasted on Dorothy than it would been on you, who collect pelvises like antlers?

JUDY: Perky. You have life again, do you.

BILLIE: Only a bit, but I'll tell you this – Hello, Dorothy.

(*DOROTHY enters.*)

JUDY: (*Leaping up and exclaiming.*) Aaah! So! How was it for you, Grandma.

DOROTHY: Why didn't anybody say it was such fun! So amusing! So out of this world, and up in the sky, so – oh, brilliant and simply not part of anything so ridiculous as one's body yet body all the way, I mean oh – it – it was – super.

JUDY: Take your arm off me.

DOROTHY: I want to touch everybody. Do we all have those surprising little places I didn't know about?

JUDY: That's enough. The mind vomits. Trevor! (*She marches out.*)

BILLIE: (*Calling.*) He doesn't want you, he doesn't want you, he doesn't want you!

JUDY: (*Off, wrenching open door.*) What the hell do you think you've been doing with that woman?

TREVOR: (*Off.*) Making love to her.

JUDY: (*Off.*) You tart. I'll show you what – (*Door slams.*)

DOROTHY: I'll have some wine, please.

ROBERT: Oh yes.

DOROTHY: It's silly to say it broadens the mind more than I expected, because it takes the mind right out of the skull and makes a great bowl of fruit out of it. And it probably improves with practice. Thank you. (*Drinks.*) It was so endless. One wanted to be everywhere, not just everywhere there, if you see what I mean, but everywhere everywhere. I mean one spread, and then curled like a nut.

ROBERT: I'd rather you didn't cry again.

BILLIE: I won't

ROBERT: No, don't.

BILLIE: No.

DOROTHY: And I love him so much, I'm so in love with him – he's so kind, sometimes one thing, sometimes another, it's like an endless dance.

BILLIE: (*Lips quivering.*) Endless?

DOROTHY: I hope so. (*Holds out glass for more drink.*)

ROBERT: What'll his parents say?

DOROTHY: I don't think that's my problem. Is it?

(*Enter JUDY, after sound of door opening and slamming.*)

JUDY: Well – well – D'you know what I've just seen? A grown man completely regressed into his childhood.

DOROTHY: We've been into that, and I'm not a mother substitute.

JUDY: Is that wine yours?

DOROTHY: Yes.

JUDY: (*Taking it.*) Don't think I care what you two get up to in his cot, I don't. (*She flings the wine in DOROTHY's face.*) And I did that because I happen not to like you. Come on, Robert, let's go out on the town.

ROBERT: No thanks, I want to stay here.

JUDY: To look after your friend Trevor?

ROBERT: To look after Billie. I'll get a cloth. (*He goes.*)

JUDY: Oh! You want Billie, Billie wants Stephen, Stephen wants out, I want Trevor, Trevor wants Dorothy –

DOROTHY: And loves her.

JUDY: In which case I really cannot bear to stay.

DOROTHY: And then there's Hugh. (*Giggles.*) He's really very nice, is Hugh.

JUDY: Like you, he's dull as ditchwater. Goodbye, and I hate you very much.

DOROTHY: Look Up, Not Down, Look Out, Not In –
no don't throw any more wine dear, it isn't nice.

TREVOR: (*Entering barefoot and with his shirt open.*) Hello.

DOROTHY: Hello!

TREVOR: You look enchanting.

JUDY: That's because you can't see her in this light, though
you did say something similar at Rupert's when we'd
finished. Goodbye.

TREVOR: I don't remember Rupert's. (*A slight giggle from
DOROTHY.*)

JUDY: It wasn't very memorable, actually.

TREVOR: Well, tonight was more than memorable. I met
another person, really and truly, and I moved into love
with her, and she was tender and surprised and revealing.
All the different bits of her life seemed to come to me in
that bed, and from now on I'll find out more and more
about her, and it'll be like light moving down empty streets
and filling them. Dorothy, you were beautiful, and you
tasted – oh, of all the salts of living.

DOROTHY: Oh, gracious.

TREVOR: I've never known what it's like to be in absolutely
the right place, home, where I belong, where I'll go on
feeling more and more right, more myself. I love you and
it's a truly original experience. I can nearly cry about it.

JUDY: Cry? I'd like to scream, I've had the most original
experience of all time, one I thought I would never have in
all my days. I have been shocked. I have been deeply and
appallingly shocked. Shocked to the bottom of my soul,
shocked where it really hurts me. Shocked, really painfully
shocked. By you two, doing all those things, shocked. So
I shan't come here again. Ever. I've had my shock and
one shock in a lifetime of that size is enough. (*She goes.*)
Goodbye.

DOROTHY: You were talking about me. Let's get some more
to drink and then come out and talk some more.
(*BILLIE cries quietly and DOROTHY puts her arms
around her as they go out.*)

Scene 9

The sounds of the pub. HUGH and HARRIET enter to ROY and JIM who have the dominoes out and three pints of beer.

ROY: Well, look at this. Should we go into the garden?

HARRIET: No, no. I haven't seen dominoes since I was a girl.

HUGH: It's fives and threes, and they don't need to play while we here talking.

JIM: We don't often get the chance to talk to people from Hugh's other life.

ROY: We never do.

JIM: Do you work with him?

HARRIET: We're just friends.

JIM: Ah, hahahahahahaha!

ROY: For God's sake Jim.

JIM: He's told us about you. I'm Jim I'm in gas, and Roy's in the construction industry.

ROY: Building. I'm a chippy when I get the chance to be.

HARRIET: I'm Harriet.

JIM: Oh! Not Dorothy?

HUGH: Dorothy's nice. And older.

ROY: What d'you do?

HARRIET: I'm in publishing, as a matter of fact. I share a flat with a girl in publishing and we have lunch every day with a girl in travel. I'm that sort of person, and I had a person like you for a father. (*This to ROY. She laughs.*) A bricky. Back to roots, eh? (*She laughs again. No-one else does.*) Oh – Get me a pint of bitter, Jim.

ROY: I'll get it.

JIM: She asked me.

ROY: You don't have to do what she says just because she's in publishing. Safe is it, in books?

HARRIET: No.

ROY: They keep the young ones, I'll be bound.

HARRIET: It's last in, first out, like everywhere.

ROY: You'll have to do real work soon, then.

HARRIET: Publishing is real work just like –

ROY: Telling us all what we ought to think, deciding what we should read, how we should all be like you –

JIM: Roy.

HARRIET: Don't talk rubbish.

ROY: You wouldn't publish a book by me, would you, but I'm the one who does most of the living round here.

JIM: You go and get the beer, then, I don't care.

ROY: Want to be the gent, do you? Want to throw your bleeding cape in the bleeding puddle, do you?

JIM: What?

HUGH: Sir Walter Raleigh – tobacco – potatoes –

JIM: I know about Sir Walter Raleigh.

ROY: You want white wine, not beer.

HARRIET: I want beer.

ROY: Wine.

HARRIET: Beer.

ROY: Wine.

HARRIET: Oh shit.

ROY: All right, beer.

HARRIET: Just sod off somewhere if you don't like me being a publisher. I sing madrigals, too, but that doesn't mean I'm some sort of class traitor who has to have white wine forced down her throat as an example to aspiring students of literature. I asked for a pint of beer, so fucking get it.

ROY: Showing your street credentials, eh?

HARRIET: Oh, for God's sake –

ROY: Yes, I'm sorry.

HARRIET: Why?

ROY: I didn't mean to be rude.

HARRIET: Yes, you did. Don't cringe.

ROY: I said what I meant. I'm sorry. It's not on to be rude.

HARRIET: Yes, all right. I'm sorry too.

JIM: (*Beginning to build a line of dominoes.*) I just think we play dominoes.

ROY: Oh Christ. It's all a mess. (*He goes out and can be heard saying.*) Mind out, I want the bar.

HUGH: What happened?

HARRIET: My aunt has landed me back into a barrow load of English resentment which no-one has yet managed to dispel.

HUGH: He's very nice usually.

HARRIET: Is he?

HUGH: I live a very peaceful, pleasant life. It doesn't have that sort of outburst in it.

JIM: Not very often.

HUGH: Never.

JIM: Well, the last time you were here, he knocked the dominoes over.

HUGH: He did? Oh, yes, he did. That was Dorothy, too.

HARRIET: What's his name, again?

HUGH: Roy.

HARRIET: Yes, it would be.

JIM: Why?

HARRIET: A publisher's silly, witty, prejudiced – It was a joke.

HUGH: Well, I don't want you to think – he was gloomy last time, wasn't he? I wonder if I've failed to notice things all these years. I wonder if I'm breaking.

JIM: (*Nervous laugh.*) Excuse me, but I think I'll –

HUGH: Sit down!

JIM: Right.

HARRIET: Did you want to go to the –

JIM: No, no, I just felt uncomfortable that was all. Ah.

(*ROY arrives with the beer.*)

ROY: One pint of beer.

HARRIET: Thanks. Cheers.

(*They all drink.*)

ROY: Obviously you're a very nice girl, and clever.

JIM: Now then, Roy.

ROY: What d'you mean, now then?

JIM: I don't mean –

ROY: Why say it, then?

JIM: It was a joke!

HUGH: What was?

JIM: Nothing. It's like a load of leaking pipes in here tonight.

HARRIET: And all because I'm in publishing, and have a randy aunt.

JIM: A randy aunt?

ROY: And, it has to be said, because you're very good-looking.

HARRIET: That's kind of you.

JIM: What's this about?

HUGH: Get on with your dominoes.

ROY: Jim's married and has children, and he's very good at it, aren't you?

JIM: I think so.

HARRIET: Are you good at it?

ROY: Not very.

HUGH: For a quiet evening in a pub we aren't half throwing round a lot of muck.

JIM: (*Still building his line of dominoes.*) I like people to think the right way.

HARRIET: So have you got work at the moment?

ROY: Yes – well, on and off.

HARRIET: Only –

ROY: Yes?

HARRIET: Nothing.

HUGH: Yes.

ROY: Yes what?

HUGH: Yes nothing. I tell you, I'm in love with a middle-aged person who is behaving very badly with a young lad. My world is falling apart, and I don't want it to fall any further, so please be careful.

JIM: Me too.

HARRIET: Is your world falling apart?

JIM: No, and I don't want it to start.

ROY: What set that off?

HUGH: I wish I'd never spoken.

ROY: When?

ROY: About the word nothing.

HARRIET: He doesn't want me to get to know you any better.

ROY: How d'you know?

HARRIET: I'm in publishing, and we read between the lines.

ROY: She just said 'only'. That's what you said, 'only', didn't you? And that set him off.

HARRIET: I have a problem in my flat. A rotten fitting. Will you come and see to it? And that, Hugh, isn't an invitation for anyone to behave uncharacteristically. I don't like romance. It's disordering, and disturbing, and to some extent disfiguring. I don't mind others having it, providing they go through it and recover. In fact, apart from my work in books the thing I give the world above all others is a helping hand through chaos, through the muddle of relationships and things like that. That is how I am a joy and a delight to my friends. Love is a game, a pleasant game and a good game to watch but I myself don't play games. Like you, Roy I work for my living, and that work matters more to me than anything else. If you could call round I would be grateful.

ROY: What is it, exactly?

HARRIET: Very suitable. French windows.

JIM: Why suitable?

HUGH: I don't know.

ROY: Nor me.

HARRIET: I did think everyone would understand that.

JIM: I'm going.

HUGH: No, stay.

JIM: I want to go.

ROY: I tell you what, Jim. Tell us what you tell the kids at bedtime, before you read to them. She'll like that.

JIM: I'm going. (*He stands. He accidentally sets the dominoes going and they fall. When they have all gone, he moves.*)

JIM: I am going now. (*He goes.*)

HUGH: I'll get some drinks. (*He leaves.*) Excuse me. Excuse me.

HARRIET: I'll give you my address.

Scene 10

Hoover. Enter MILLY. Turns off Hoover.

MILLY: And if they do sell it, they'll keep me on as a guard dog, don't care who the buyers are, though I have my suspicions.

(*DOROTHY enters.*)

DOROTHY: Milly!

MILLY: Oh, so you've come. What happened to Thursday? (*GORDON begins his shuffling entry. He has no socks on.*)

DOROTHY: Milly, I'm going on a sort of honeymoon.

MILLY: She'll be pleased to hear that, oh yes, it's all right for some.

DOROTHY: I simply came to say that after today, I won't be seeing her for a bit, and even then, not quite so often.

MILLY: You're not pregnant?

DOROTHY: No!

MILLY: Good, because she's had a fall and we've been trying to reach you.

DOROTHY: No! How?

MILLY: Thursday came and went without the usual visit, so she took it into her head to go out after tea, and, of course, naturally, as she would, she fell. It's possible she may be all right.

DOROTHY: Thank God.

MILLY: But she may not.

DOROTHY: I'll go and see her now, but Milly, I'm going to have my honeymoon.

MILLY: Who's paying for it?

DOROTHY: Me.

MILLY: And who'll pay for your mother?

DOROTHY: No-one has to pay.

MILLY: But if they do? A nursing home for instance?

DOROTHY: It's not that bad is it?

MILLY: And who's to look after her here? Me again?

DOROTHY: You've got the pension book.

MILLY: Oh yes, I keep her clean, all of them, I keep them clean, and I'm telling you, your mother can be a pretty nasty sight if she doesn't reach the toilet. I sometimes think it's the geriatric ward for her, if they'll take her, although of course, with your new – is it partner? – you might like to become full-time carers.

DOROTHY: Well I – no, I don't think we would, but in the meantime, I'm sure you're tremendously capable.

GORDON: She's a dirty-minded old witch. And your mother wants you, Dorothy.

MILLY: You mind what you're saying, Gordon. I know you and your Scottish name. But where did your ancestors come from?

GORDON: Where?

MILLY: He's a clever little Jewboy. I've felt things about him that have told me. (*She hoovers frantically.*)

DOROTHY: Stop. Stop!

GORDON: Stop!

(*She does.*)

GORDON: What does she mean?

DOROTHY: If I hear you saying racist things again, I'll report you.

MILLY: Who to?

DOROTHY: The warden.

MILLY: If there is one. Suppose they sell it all? To the Jewboys?

DOROTHY: They won't sell it to any boys. Now wash your mouth out and get Gordon some socks. (*She leaves.*)

MILLY: You see what sex does to people?

GORDON: I see what lack of it does. My Hugh's very depressed, No, stay away. Stay away! You molesting old bugger! (*He pulls away from her and she goes out hoovering and shouting.*)

MILLY: I may be the one who selects you all! It may be down to me! Oh, yes! It may be down to me! (*Leaves.*)
(*There is a sudden silence. GORDON, alone on the stage, listens.*)

GORDON: Someone's pulled her plug out. There's a few years in you yet, Gordon and you don't have to give in to anything. Just remember we're all awkward, and that's the beauty of it. (*He gives a wheezy laugh and exits.*)

Scene 11

Enter MARIE in a wheelchair being pushed by HUGH. She is covered in a rug.

HUGH: Where did it happen?

MARIE: There, where the roses were. There's a crevice. Hah.

HUGH: We must get that seen to.

MARIE: Oh, I don't think I can stay here now. You're out if you can't look after yourself.

HUGH: Can't you buy your place?

MARIE: No. Dorothy had the bulk of the money when he died, which we thought right. She's always been very good, visiting, and there's Milly, keeps my pension and lies to the warden that I'm healthy. But I can't buy in.

HUGH: Oh. And she's got a toyboy now. (*Laughs.*) And she missed seeing you, Thursday.

MARIE: I did this myself, Hugh.

HUGH: You're a very independent lady, but you mustn't take the blame for others.

MARIE: Will you buy Gordon's flat for him?

HUGH: What?

(*Enter DOROTHY.*)

DOROTHY: Oh Mother, Mother, what are they going to do?

MARIE: Doctor says rest, and I've told him I don't want a new hip. (*To HUGH.*) Why aren't you with Gordon, discussing things?

GORDON: (*Appearing.*) Because I'm coming out.

MARIE: Oh heck.

GORDON: And why aren't you with me?

HUGH: I just came upon Dorothy's mother in the passage. Good afternoon, Dorothy.

DOROTHY: Good afternoon Hugh.

GORDON: You were going to see the warden.

HUGH: She was out.

GORDON: County Hall, County Hall! They're up to something.

MARIE: How's love?

DOROTHY: Why didn't you tell me it was wonderful?

MARIE: Something else you can blame me for. And it isn't always.

GORDON: I didn't get a chair when I fell in the roses.

MARIE: You're a man.

GORDON: You pushed me.

MARIE: I never.

GORDON: And my Hugh's gone all silent.

DOROTHY: It's me and my boy friend. I've brought him for you to meet, Mother. Shall I get him?

MARIE: We may as well have a look at him.

DOROTHY: (*Going.*) He's beautiful. Just remember that, he's beautiful.

GORDON: He's out of work, isn't he?

HUGH: His friend says he can get him a job, in tea.

MARIE: Picking it?

HUGH: Selling it.

MARIE: That'll mean he becomes independent. He might not want her then. Or me.

GORDON: Are you going to buy my flat or am I going to come and live with you?

HUGH: Nothing's settled Dad.

GORDON: Bloody hell, I'm in that crevice. Get me out.

(*HUGH goes to help but stops as DOROTHY and TREVOR enter.*)

DOROTHY: Here he is, Trevor. My mother, Gordon, Hugh's father – the rose bushes.

TREVOR: Hello, Hello.

MARIE: Are you going to marry her?

DOROTHY: Mother!

TREVOR: I haven't asked her yet.

MARIE: Do you have parents?

TREVOR: They're both quite young, in their fifties.

GORDON: We're half dead. Get me out.

MARIE: You know what I'm thinking, I suppose.

TREVOR: Yes.

GORDON: She's thinking you'll have to look after her if they close this place, or she gets worse. Pull.

HUGH: Wait, Father.

TREVOR: I'm in love with Dorothy and if you want to come and live with us –

HUGH: Won't you want children?

TREVOR: We've only known each other three days.

HUGH: But she's past it –

DOROTHY: Oh for goodness' sake! All this talk in public! I'm so embarrassed!

MARIE: You're very middle-aged, Dorothy. Give us all a sweetie, Gordon, to celebrate.

GORDON: No.

MARIE: (*To HUGH.*) He hides them in his pocket.

GORDON: What are we celebrating? Give over!

MARIE: I like him. And they're going to live together. And I might live with them.

DOROTHY: No.

TREVOR: Why not?

DOROTHY: She'd drive us mad. And I couldn't go romping about the house stark naked with the woman responsible for my birth watching me.

MARIE: Don't be feeble.

DOROTHY: If I'm feeble, it's your fault.

MARIE: (*Imitating.*) If I'm feeble it's your fault – Ah! (*DOROTHY is about to hit her.*) You can't hit me in this chair, can you?

TREVOR: Dorothy! She's your mother and she's defenceless.

DOROTHY: Don't you see?

MARIE: Get me to the loo, someone.

(*GORDON goes over.*)

GORDON: Aaah! You did that, rummaging for sweeties.

HUGH: I didn't.

MARIE: The loo, the toilet, quick!

TREVOR: I'll take you.

DOROTHY: I'll see to it.

TREVOR: You go and help the old gentleman. This way, mother-in-law.

MARIE: You'll have to wipe my bum.

TREBVOR: (*Pushing her out.*) Okay.

DOROTHY: (*Screaming.*) I'm so embarrassed!

HUGH: Then help me get him up! Come!

GORDON: I've broken. And I want a chair like that.

HUGH: That's why you did it, you old monster.

GORDON: (*As they lift him.*) No, I didn't.

HUGH: Yes, you did.

GORDON: No, I didn't.

HUGH: Oh yes, you did,

GORDON: Oh no, I didn't. (*Screams. As they carry him off he screams more.*)

DOROTHY: Get an ambulance. Milly, someone, get an ambulance! He's broken something.

HUGH: If this is what love does, it's a complete nuisance.

Scene 12

The two gardens. Evening. Music coming from HARRIET's flat. She comes out into the garden with ROY.

ROY: Who was that?

HARRIET: A lady collecting for the Romanian orphans. There's the rot.

ROY: I'll have to get it all out and replace the window, a whole day's job, next week. Shall I take a key, or will you wait in for me?

HARRIET: Why should I wait in for you?

ROY: I might try to steal mementoes. I'm poleaxed by you, and you know it.

HARRIET: Oh, don't be trite.

ROY: I'll go.

HARRIET: No. Talk.

ROY: What can I talk about when all I'm doing is passing the time till you begin to feel able to do it with me? It's all a bugger – Why did you ask me to come?

HARRIET: Oh dear. How helpless one suddenly becomes when one actually falls for another fleshly lump. The books I read say 'If you fall in love, you can't help it, but you can choose to go on falling in love, or to stop. Love,' say the books, etching pictures of solitary heroes from the myths of the American West, 'is riding off into the sunset all alone- letting go, they call it – or it's what you do with your partner when you have no feelings at all. It's commitment, not feeling. Duty, not passion.' How awful to say that, to urge pretence, to summon up the cold shower. I've believed it all for several impregnable years, but I know, when I feel this maddening lust out in the garden – and there's honeysuckle, I notice, somewhere – when I squirm with this celestial hunger for another particular embodied person that to speak of duty, which is what you fall back on when everything else is dead as winter, that is to ask for schoolmaster stuff to hold the headlong Gods in check. All right Roy, I'm sure we're into father figures and Freud all over the place, upward mobility, nostalgie de la boue. Who cares. All I know is, I've never gone like this, and there's endless trouble looming. Let's make love, and let's make love now, and then regret it all like hell if we have to.

ROY: You're saying something only an idiot would think of in that way. I'm married.

HARRIET: If you're suggesting we sing madrigals instead –

ROY: I'm going to get divorced.

HARRIET: For me?

ROY: Who else?

HARRIET: But we've only – does this happen?

ROY: Yes. It's a wasps' nest. Come along and turn off that music. Where's the bedroom?

(*They go off and the music stops as ROBERT comes out into the garden in his office clothes and goes straight to the boundary between the two gardens.*)

ROBERT: Billie! Billie, where are you? Billie?

(*Enter from the same side TREVOR and DOROTHY.*)

DOROTHY: It's no good, Trevor. You're young, you've got a job, you'll have money, and you've got proper parents. You don't need me.

ROBERT: Hello.

(*The bell goes.*)

TREVOR: I don't need but I want you.

(*Bell again.*)

DOROTHY: That's not enough.

ROBERT: I'll get it. We've an envelope for the Romanian orphans. (*He goes.*)

TREVOR: Your mother's right. You don't want freedom. You want your little house in Luton, to hide in and feel gloomy.

DOROTHY: No I don't.

TREVOR: I want to live with you. Are you, or are you not going to do it?

DOROTHY: It's all so complicated.

(*Enter ROBERT with wine and HUGH.*)

HUGH: I'm not very sorry to interrupt you, since you practically slammed the door in my face, but I wish it to be perfectly clear that I wish to marry Dorothy. My father is now in hospital for a considerable period of time, and so I want to settle down with her and live happily ever after, hahaha.

ROBERT: Wine. (*He starts to pour it.*)

HUGH: She's had her late adolescence, so now she can look forward to the grassy uplands.

DOROTHY: No.

TREVOR: Great.

DOROTHY: If you expect me to give up all this for the long, dry twilight of retired insurance conversation, you must be mad.

TREVOR: Wonderful.

DOROTHY: But nonetheless, we have to be realistic, Trevor.

HUGH: Yes. He's a young man, and that's the whole thing about this.

TREVOR: Realistic is an entirely subjective word. Will you marry me?

DOROTHY: I want so much to, oh I do, but you're so stupid not to see the difficulties.

(*Into the next garden come JUDY and BILLIE, BILLIE howling.*)

TREVOR: Oh God, shut up!

JUDY: It's not because of Stephen this time. She's been threatened with redundancy.

BILLIE: But only because I wasn't concentrating because I was thinking of Stephen, so it's all the same thing –

ROBERT: Then why don't you bloody well stop thinking about him and get on with your work!

BILLIE: What?

ROBERT: I'm sorry.

BILLIE: No. I'm, sorry.

ROBERT: What for?

BILLIE: I've no idea.

ROBERT: Will you marry me?

BILLIE: No. (*But there are no tears.*)

JUDY: I'm vacant.

ROBERT: No thanks.

JUDY: What's wrong with you? Neither of you knows a proper woman when you see one, do you. It's these dreadful needy sisters in adversity that fascinate you.

DOROTHY: I'm not needy.

BILLIE: I am, but I'm not going to show it. I can't afford to get the sack.

TREVOR: Well, Dorothy and I are getting married.

DOROTHY: No, we're not.

TREVOR: As soon as she feels up to it.

HUGH: This is very foolish.

JUDY: It's mad! Mad, mad, mad!

DOROTHY: And we're not doing it!

> (*BILLIE cries*
> *Enter HARRIET and ROY.*)

ROY: We're trying to fuck in here.

HUGH: Roy! What on earth will Jim say?

ROBERT: Who's Jim?

HARRIET: He plays dominoes.

HUGH: I'm surprised at you. I'm surprised at all of you, especially the educated ones.

HARRIET: We're getting married, Hugh. Roy's getting divorced and we're getting married.

JUDY: I never expected to be the only one who wasn't having a love affair, but thank goodness I'm not doing that. Marriage is like a zip fastener that falls apart whenever you do it up, and I hate having broken things around the house.

BILLIE: Dorothy, you did all this. Aren't you going to finish it properly and marry Trevor?

HUGH: No!

DOROTHY: He'll tire of me.

TREVOR: You're scared.

HARRIET: Madrigals, then?

TREVOR: Don't you love me?

DOROTHY: Oh yes, I love you.

TREVOR: That's it, then.

DOROTHY: All right then, that is it, I love him and I'm going to teach him everything, absolutely everything there is to know about me, and I'm going to learn everything there is to know about him. And learning those things we shall adore them, and respect them, and stand away from them, and plunge into them again and again – oh, we'll love each other, fight each other, never harm each other and in there (*Gestures to indoors.*) we'll do such things – and then go shopping.

JUDY: Oh, roll over Luton, welcome Tescos –

DOROTHY: And we'll do the washing up, and the gardening, and know exactly what to buy for each other's birthdays –

ROY: If that's that, Harriet and I have one or two things to finish off.

JUDY: No, no, no. Dear friends, I've slept with Trevor, and it was very sweet. But I've slept with lots of people. And girls like me are dangerous nowadays.

DOROTHY: You mean – you're –

TREVOR: Positive?

JUDY: I've no idea, and I don't intend to find out.

DOROTHY: (*Getting a chair.*) If you've killed the only man I've ever loved, the one person, the only person who showed me how to leave myself behind, I'm going to beat you insensible! (*She is on the chair and trying to climb over into the next garden.*)

TREVOR: Dorothy!

DOROTHY: (*To TREVOR.*) Are you – have you –

TREVOR: I don't know. (*To JUDY.*) Christ, you little tart.

DOROTHY: Yes. No! You too.

TREVOR: Me?

DOROTHY: You loved each other for a second or so. You must've done, carried away beyond – So don't be angry, anyone. Your lives have been sharp – I would like very much to have lived them myself. In that way, it doesn't quite matter. And now it's happened, or perhaps has happened, you and I know that no-one can take away the things we've found during these few days – don't we? (*TREVOR nods.*)

DOROTHY: So if we let them go, then that's our doing, not anyone else's, not any illness, not even my mother. Oh – let's love each other, every way, whether we're dying or not, so we can forget we've ever been nice. I hope you're negative, Judy, for your sake as well as ours, but just for now, buzz off will you? We've got everything, and haven't long to use it in.

HUGH: I've got a pension.

(*MILLY and the unidentified man appear once again in some remote place.*)

MILLY: Well, are you selling or aren't you?

MAN: We haven't decided yet. I know it hurts to be kept on the rack of indecision, madame, but there we are.

MILLY: Bloody hell, bloody hell, bloody bloody hell.

HARRIET: Roy?

ROY: Be strong love.

TREVOR: My really nice Dorothy. I love you. (*They hug.*)

(*MILLY screams and beats her fists.*
JUDY paces up and down.
BILLIE and ROBERT reach across the divide.)

The End.

THE LAST THRASH

Characters

HENRY
A clean young man, aged twenty-five. Games.

ADELAIDE
A maiden lady in her fifties, always with a lesson planning book.
English.

MARTIN
A single man of thirty-five, baggy, thinning hair. Latin.

CATTLEY
'Catfish', forty-nine, single, charming.
French and Deputy Headmaster.

MONTY
Married, late fifties, rather heavy. Maths.

MRS MORRISON
Upper thirties, blonde, and rich.
Youthful good taste. Parent.

JERRY MORRISON
A thirteen-year-old boy. Her son, and a pupil.

KAY
Late twenties, very trim. School secretary.

JANICE
Colourful in contemporary ways. Art.

HERBERT
Wears a suit, late fifties. The Headmaster.

The play is set on the Staff Lawn of Chantrey's Preparatory School for Boys in the South of England, and it is in two acts covering eighteen sunny, and moonlit, hours at the end of the summer term.

The Last Thrash was first performed at The Orange Tree Theatre, Richmond, on 28 April 1999, with the following cast:

HENRY, Nick Fletcher

ADELAIDE, Tricia Kelly

MARTIN, Paul Kemp

JOHN CATTLEY, Jeremy Crutchley

MONTY, David Timson

MRS MORRISON, Lucy Tregear

JERRY MORRISON, George Belfield and Sam Marks

KAY, Emma Gregory

JANICE, Sarah Tansey

HERBERT, Sam Walters

Director, Dominic Hill

Designer, Tim Meacock

Lighting Designer, Jonathan Rowland

Assistant Director, Richard Cullen

Fight Director, Alison de Burgh

Stage Manager, Annabel FitzGerald

Props, Matt Turner and Clair Parker

Set Construction, Simon Lally and Jonathan Rowland

Production Photographer, Sheila Burnett

ACT ONE

*The scene throughout is a lawn with several seats scattered over it.
There is an entry from one side from a building and an entry from
the other side from the general direction of a school playing field.
There is the shadow of a tree over all. At the moment a man in
his early twenties, dressed as a batsman in cricket gear, HENRY,
is addressing the grass rather vehemently.*

HENRY: Oh lawn! Oh lovely staff-room lawn! Oh great
horse chestnut and splendid Victorian Gothic! Oh bursting twelve-year-olds and smell of gym shoes in the ancient
countryside!
(*A middle-aged woman, ADELAIDE, enters from the
building. As always, she carries, a lesson-planning book
with her. She has been listening.*)
ADELAIDE: Are you being poetic or disturbed?
HENRY: I'm so at home in a prep school, and I dread the
summer holidays.
ADELAIDE: You do still have Patricia to absorb whatever it is?
HENRY: Oh yes.
ADELAIDE: Of course, she is in London, which isn't instantly
available. (*Sitting.*) Go on.
HENRY: Oh tree, Christmas will be fabulous because I'm
taking the rugger tour to France, if I can find just one more
prep school in the Alpes Maritimes, but – how I hate the
smell of summer and the end of life.
ADELAIDE: Life returns to beautiful normality in September,
Henry, with the leaves.
(*Voices are heard off shouting 'Oh!' and 'Shot!' and clap-
ping as a cricket ball bounces onto the lawn.*)
HENRY: Heavens! That must be Monty.
BOY'S VOICE OFF: Sir?
HENRY: Here, Rupert. (*He throws the ball back.*)
BOY'S VOICE OFF: Thank you, sir
HENRY: Fancy Monty scoring a six.
ADELAIDE: He hates cricket and he hates the staff match,
so he gets savage. Go on.

HENRY: On? Oh lucky boys who actually are going home.

ADELAIDE: They're not. They're leaving home, heading for divorces and elliptical conversations.

HENRY: There's a treacly smell of youth everywhere. I feel sick.

ADELAIDE: It's death.

HENRY: Death?

(*Enter from the building MARTIN, a slightly portly man with thinning hair, aged about thirty-five, though he will never look any different. He is also dressed for batting and is reading a letter aloud to himself. It is written on blue paper.*)

MARTIN: Darling Bobby. Does your golden hair still glimmer in the corridors of Uppingham? Are you still the burnished lad who –

HENRY: Oh God!

MARTIN: (*Looking up.*) What?

ADELAIDE: Give that to me, Martin.

MARTIN: (*Hiding it.*) I'm learning the words of Linden Lea for the end of term concert.

ADELAIDE: Do you send those things to Bobby Thomas often?

MARTIN: Never. I write each day, but I flush them down the loo, and the head has had a word, and since they're not on school note paper, it's all right.

HENRY: Oh God, oh God!

MARTIN: You don't like me do you!

HENRY: No!

ADELAIDE: (*Cross.*) Of course he does, we all do, there's no room for anything else!

(*JANICE, the twenty-year-old art teacher, has entered. She is dressed in bright and possibly clashing colours. She enters from the field with a sketch pad.*)

JANICE: More love letters to Bobby?

ADELAIDE: Sh!

MARTIN: It's Linden Lea.

JANICE: Oh really.

MARTIN: Yes!

(*JANICE continues offstage into the building.*)

JANICE: There's no point in ogling me, Henry, even though I sketched you at the crease.

HENRY: I'm not ogling.

ADELAIDE: (*Calling.*) The Art Department talks too much!

HENRY: I'm going back to the match.

MARTIN: Go on, then, go!

HENRY: Right.

VOICES OFFSTAGE: 'Oh, well done!' (*Clapping.*)

MARTIN: (*As another ball drops in.*) Heavens!

HENRY: (*Picking up the ball.*) What on earth's got into Monty?

ADELAIDE: (*Herself angry.*) Rage!

MARTIN: Were you two talking?

(*JOHN CATTLEY appears from the building side, unnoticed by the others, as HENRY leaves, preparing to throw the ball back. CATTLEY is tall, late forties, sallow and smooth.*)

HENRY: Rupert?

BOY'S VOICE: Sir.

HENRY: (*Leaving to the field and to throw the ball.*) That's my boy.

CATTLEY: His boy?

ADELAIDE: (*Cross.*) He's being affectionate.

MARTIN: We're all affectionate! And the head has had a word.

CATTLEY: What about?

MARTIN: How well I teach Latin, which I do, because I love it, and I'm going to the pavilion to help with tea. (*He leaves.*)

CATTLEY: (*Following, calling.*) You are good at teaching Latin, Martin.

MARTIN: (*Off.*) I know!

CATTLEY: (*Off.*) I only want to calm you down.

ADELAIDE: (*Calling.*) We're all good at teaching, so concentrate on that! (*To the audience.*) What do they think we're here for?

(*Enter MORRISON from the building side, dressed for cricket and thirteen years old.*)

Morrison? This is the staff lawn and you should be fielding.

MORRISON: The head wanted a word, Miss.

ADELAIDE: You look unhappy.

MORRISON: No, Miss.

ADELAIDE: Yes, you do, Jerry. Come. There. There, there, there.

MORRISON: Can I go, please?

ADELAIDE: Is it something bad?

MORRISON: My mother's out there.

ADELAIDE: Well, she's a nice lady, isn't she?
   (*CATTLEY returns.*)

MORRISON: Yes.

ADELAIDE: Good. And remember, I'm always here.
   (*MORRISON leaves to the field, passing CATTLEY.*)

MORRISON: Excuse me, sir.

CATTLEY: Always here? Are you all right?

ADELAIDE: Martin's a hazard, Henry's going funny, but I'm all right. I don't know about the others.

CATTLEY: It's the end of term.

ADELAIDE: I know it is!

CATTLEY: Then don't snap at me!

ADELAIDE: (*Near angry tears.*) Well, they're so nice! I shall go and say useful things to the mothers. (*She leaves.*)

CATTLEY: (*To the audience.*) My name is Cattley, Deputy Head, and the boys call me Catfish behind my back. I love that. Nicknames mean they have you inside them, and I like them saying it behind my back because that means they respect what I stand for. I stand for – we stand for – class. By that I don't mean anything sociological – that would be silly nowadays, especially as we have trade union children here. Rupert. (*Light laugh.*) No, I mean discrimination, sorting out the best. I love, I love the best. The parents have to pay good cash for it, of course, but not because of snobbery. They genuinely do believe that if you pay for things you get a better quality of life, somehow grow nearer the throne. So what we do here, what I do here, is gently break the children in at ten or eleven for a life without Mummy and Daddy so they become achievers, masters of the great world, putting higher things, ideals, in place of home. I suppose – I often say this, and it's true, it

144

is true – I suppose we, very gently, damage them, but only to improve them to a new, true direction. We give them life with Catfish, me, Deputy Head of Chantrey's Preparatory School for Boys, to inspire them to real life. And they just love it. Oh yes, they can play golf – we're very modern here, we've a computer centre – or phone home if they want to. And if they persist in being miserable, then after lights out they can sob themselves to sleep, or learn to masturbate in preparation for the great public schools.

VOICES OFF: 'Oh, well caught!' (*Clapping.*)

CATTLEY: I give my life to this enormous cause because I so much want them to be happy. Dear God, I want them to be happy, and with that deep inner happiness that comes from strength and a hugely contributive life. Therefore they leave here knowing that not only can they survive but they can conquer, and carry always –
(*Enter MONTY from the field, wearing pads with his cricket gear. He is in his fifties. He is preparing to light a cigarette.*)

MONTY: There's someone coming.

CATTLEY: (*Of the cigarette.*) Put that away.

MONTY: I've scored two sixes.

CATTLEY: Who is it?

MONTY: Your dream of a better life.

CATTLEY: I don't have dreams like that.

MONTY: They say you do.

CATTLEY: Who does?

MONTY: Everyone.

CATTLEY: You're a loose cannon, Monty.

MONTY: I teach a very firm Pythagoras.

CATTLEY: (*Peering.*) It's Mrs Morrison.

MONTY: The great outside approaches.
(*Enter MRS MORRISON from the playing field wearing jeans and a smart simple top and earrings. Late thirties and very attractive.*)

MRS MORRISON: (*Smiling.*) Mr Cattley. Hullo.

CATTLEY: Mrs Morrison. What a beautiful surprise.

MRS MORRISON: (*To MONTY.*) Do smoke if you want to.

MONTY: No, no, it's –

CATTLEY: To what do we owe this pleasure?

MRS MORRISON: I'm looking for Jerry. He left the field, someone said, and I wondered –

MONTY: He came back and caught me out.

CATTLEY: He's very good at cricket.

MONTY: He's very good at trigonometry.

CATTLEY: He's very good at everything.

MRS MORRISON: But not head boy.

MONTY: Odd that.

MRS MORRISON: I thought so.

CATTLEY: Do sit down. Since Jerry's back on the field now, we can talk more about the pyramid outside the Louvre. Can I persuade you to dally with us?

MRS MORRISON: I think I ought to watch Jerry playing, actually, but any time you're passing the farm – mm. (*This sound is affirmative.*)

CATTLEY: I might actually do that, later in the day.

MRS MORRISON: Then call – mm. (*Goes.*) I like the pyramid outside the Louvre.

MONTY: The great outside retires. And, bad luck, she likes the pyramid outside the Louvre.

CATTLEY: If you're going to smoke that, Monty, please do it in the Common Room

MONTY: (*Cross.*) You're so trivial. Why wasn't Morrison head boy?

CATTLEY: It's a bit late to ask.

MONTY: But I am asking.

CATTLEY: Then don't.

(*KAY enters from the building.*)

Ah! The school secretary.

MONTY: Availability always counts for more than dreams, of course. (*He goes into the building.*

KAY is the sensible and attractive school secretary in her twenties.)

KAY: I didn't understand him.

CATTLEY: What is it?

KAY: There's a problem with Morrison.

CATTLEY: Again?

KAY: And the Head wants a word.

CATTLEY: You look like a tiger cub.

KAY: Morrison's been back to the village. You look like a lion.

CATTLEY: Tiger you.

KAY: Lion you. Anyway, the shop's rung up again, and the Head –

CATTLEY: The Head! How the masochist in him loves it when I shout my challenge! 'Headmaster,' I cry, 'although the boy has visited the village shop so often he must've bought it up by now, with due respect, Headmaster, with due respect I do just wonder what the fuck does it matter?' He loves to hear that as he squirms and wriggles. 'What the fuck does it matter?'

KAY: He suspects Morrison went to buy cannabis.

CATTLEY: Oh – Lord. I suppose he's panicking about publicity, though with Henry's future father-in-law owning half the nation's press he's got an ally.

KAY: If Henry marries her.

CATTLEY: Jokes on TV and grave discussions with the parents – (*He looks off.*) Sweet Kay, dear friendly, sensible Kay – it is the end of term and I am tense.

KAY: He's noticed us, too. He says I've got a Birmingham accent.

CATTLEY: Have you ever had your heart broken?

KAY: John – our holiday in Normandy –

CATTLEY: I just wondered if you'd known that very maturing experience.

KAY: I don't want to pre-empt your thinking.

CATTLEY: No. I must go and see the –

KAY: You really want a person who can think as much as you, don't you.

CATTLEY: I'm a teacher. There aren't people who can think as much as I do.

(*Enter the HEADMASTER, HERBERT, preserving gravitas and wearing a suit.*)

HEADMASTER: John –

CATTLEY: Headmaster.

HEADMASTER: I'd like a word.

CATTLEY: I'm told you've had a word with our resident
 paederast.

HEADMASTER: Miss Hammerstone –

CATTLEY: So perhaps you'll have one soon with Henry,
 because he's going funny.

HEADMASTER: What?

CATTLEY: According to Adelaide, who has menopausal
 difficulties which –

HEADMASTER: Language!

CATTLEY: Do we have a wacky baccy problem?

HEADMASTER: You can go, Miss Hammerstone.

CATTLEY: No.

HEADMASTER: She is simply the school secretary, and –

CATTLEY: I'll tell her everything you say within five minutes.

HEADMASTER: Has the end of term brought on one of your
 democratic moods?

(*CATTLEY smiles and says nothing.*)

KAY: Yes, it has.

HEADMASTER: You'd know of course. Well, then, Morrison.
 What Morrison has done, Mr Cattley, and I want to make
 it very clear to you, and since she's still here, to Miss
 Hammerstone also, is this. He has broken the school rules.
 He has visited the village shop, which he is only allowed
 to do on Wednesday and Saturday afternoons, and he
 has consistently done it on Thursdays, and this time on
 Fridays, too. In his cricket clothes. The day of the staff
 match. With his mother here. I trust you recognise dumb
 insolence when you see it?

(*CATTLEY smiles and says nothing.*)

KAY: Yes, he does.

HEADMASTER: The battle of Waterloo was not won by
 people visiting the village shop on Thursdays and Fridays
 and that is the point of this institution, so don't go rambling
 on about initiative and care for the individual.

KAY: It's in the brochure. I read the brochure. I'm the school
 secretary.

HEADMASTER: We're talking here about rotten apples, not
 initiative and you know quite well, John, that the Morri-
 sons want their child to be clever but usual, so don't taunt

me with your condescending views – yes, you do, you do,
you know you do, and I enjoy it over sherry, but not now.
I'm sending Morrison home early.

(*CATTLEY raises his eyebrows and says nothing.*)

HEADMASTER: And don't get psychological. I'm sending
him home, yes, home, as a punishment. It'll go on his
report as well, so I'm afraid Winchester –

KAY: Has he admitted the drugs?

HEADMASTER: Of course not. He denies everything.

KAY: What else could he do?

HEADMASTER: Confess and take his punishment like a man.
That's what we teach them, and the world admires us for it.

KAY: But if he's innocent –

HEADMASTER: The shop identified him.

KAY: They sold him cannabis?

HEADMASTER: Don't be silly, shops aren't like that. I'm
talking to the Deputy Headmaster and I'm telling him that
I'm punishing dumb insolence, and that is the skill the
parents pay me for. I simply thought he smelt funny.

KAY: They all do, it's nice.

CATTLEY: Monty gets his ganja in a coppice just behind the –

HEADMASTER: Don't torture me!

CATTLEY: I don't!

HEADMASTER: You do, you do, you know you do!

CATTLEY: Yes, I do!

HEADMASTER: Yes!

CATTLEY: I'm sorry! I'm sorry that I torture you. I am. I'm
sorry. I believe – I do believe – this is a good place, and it
works beautifully, and I love the things that we reveal to
the young minds that come here.

HEADMASTER: Yes.

CATTLEY: To see the first dawning of wonder at a piece of
Mozart, or the sudden mastery of a French construction –

HEADMASTER: Yes, all right.

CATTLEY: – and to know that all that splendour is going out
into the world in those young heads with all the power to
influence ways of being, and shape them in the image of
that excellence –

HEADMASTER: Yes, I know.

CATTLEY: – those are truly sweet pleasures for a man, among the sweetest and most perfect one can think of.

HEADMASTER: Right.

CATTLEY: I utterly relish, swallow almost whole, the work we do here.

KAY: Yes!

HEADMASTER: Don't be taken in. He's a liberal.

CATTLEY: And because of that work, I give my life to your school. But – I do have to say, I really do, that when it comes to visiting the village shop, Headmaster, with due respect, with all due respect, I do just wonder what the –

HEADMASTER: Then don't wonder! No-one must find out about Martin and Monty and Morrison because there's more at stake than you know, and I will tell you what it is just as soon as it's confirmed from places I'm allowed to mention.

CATTLEY: What places?

HEADMASTER: Shush! And since we're all three together, no-one certainly must find out now about your intimacy with Miss Hammerstein – stone! Hammerstone.

CATTLEY: Why did you call her that?

HEADMASTER: Did I?

KAY: You know my name quite well.

CATTLEY: What is this?

HEADMASTER: You know quite well what it is. I don't allow intimacy on the premises. Now, I've had a word, so –

KAY: We love each other. Mr Cattley?

HEADMASTER: You have a Birmingham accent and the parents don't expect to hear a Birmingham accent when they're paying twelve thousand pounds per annum for –

CATTLEY: She's never seen Birmingham.

HEADMASTER: We must be whiter than white, especially if I'm going to punish the child of a well-known local personage and make him believe my version of events and not his son's. And at this moment, I can't have people saying things about us, just when certain other people are making up their minds whether or not –

CATTLEY: What's this got to do with Kay's name?

HEADMASTER: I can't have people of a certain sort carrying on with my staff in public like –

CATTLEY: She's not a person of a certain sort.

KAY: We love each other, tell him.

CATTLEY: Kay and I have a healthy love of sensuality, she
especially. She comes on top, underneath, uses her tongue
like a whip, rolls her hips until you scream, presents
buttocks like the limpid moons of Jupiter, swallows things
in breathless gulps –

HEADMASTER: Silence!

KAY: I didn't mean you to say that!

HEADMASTER: Someone may be listening.

CATTLEY: I know you, Herbert. Should rumour reach the
outside world of this great celebration of the Fleurs du Mal,
to satisfy the prudish parents you'd get rid of her, her, not
me and you'd do it because you'd persuaded yourself –
and put it about in filthy little hints – that she's somehow
cheap, dirty, nasty, for instance what you'd call an upstart
Birmingham Jewess –

HEADMASTER: Shush!

CATTLEY: – a person certain British standards will not tolerate, of whom no more could be expected –

HEADMASTER: Please!

CATTLEY: – even though you take good money from people
of whom exactly that description frequently passes your lips.

KAY: Oh God.

HEADMASTER: I usually take it from the grandparents.

CATTLEY: Our bodies go like mountain streams in drenches
of wet excitement that even the staff match cannot equal,
and it is wonderful.

HEADMASTER: We are bringing up the rulers of the world
here, and very soon it's possible –

CATTLEY: Like Morrison?

HEADMASTER: Whose mother is so different from a school
secretary. Aha. Ahaahaaha!

KAY: Pardon?

HEADMASTER: What I shall do now is send Morrison home
tomorrow. Quite possibly I shall also thrash him.

KAY: For buying sweets?

CATTLEY: Thrashing is illegal.

HEADMASTER: We don't know if it was just buying sweets, do we, and if was drugs, thrashing will teach him a real lesson, legal or not, and his mother signed a disclaimer to say that I could beat him if I thought it necessary and I do. It says I can do it in the brochure, even if it's in very small print and out of date – no, no, don't say another thing.

CATTLEY: It's illegal.

HEADMASTER: But I can threaten him. We're independent here, John, we don't kowtow to anyone, and if we think it's right to protect moral values by thrashing, then thrashing's what we'll do, or threaten to do, and keep your noisy conscience to yourself.

CATTLEY: It's against the law, independent or not. Don't you understand? The law?

HEADMASTER: The law says – let's be very clear about this – that we can thrash pupils – or touch them, anyway – to save them from injury, and taking drugs is injury, so I would be saving Morrison from himself if I thrashed him, which I might, and certainly feel like doing.

CATTLEY: You'd be prosecuted, the school would close, our ideals would evaporate –

HEADMASTER: Who'd betray me? The staff are loyal, the boys are loyal, the parents think that a good beating never hurt anyone – they all signed up to it once, like Morrison's mother. Now, just do your job, stop salivating over the school secretary, go and speak to Mrs Morrison for me, explain how very good it would be if her son were thrashed if he had to be, which he probably won't, and persuade her to recommend us to as many of her friends as possible, which she will do when she hears the news I can't begin to tell you.

CATTLEY: What news?

HEADMASTER: I can't begin to tell you. Go on, she's down there at the match and your tongue is silky and you fancy her – yes, you do, you do, I know you do, aha ahaahaahah – having drinks in her delicious conversion? Go on. Discipline is your job, morality is your job, I pay you to be good, transparently good, and goodness is rules, which

Morrison has broken, and this school will not tolerate that, it can't afford to, none of us can, times being what they are, no more assisted places and a sort of Labour government, so don't argue. Just do your job, be suave and save us all. Right. Good. And be dignified. This is a seat of learning. (*He leaves. To KAY as he goes.*) You watch your step. We're going to take in girls here soon. Nice ones.

CATTLEY: (*Shouting to him offstage.*) I have to say, 'What the fuck does it matter?'

(*Offstage clapping.*)

VOICES OFF: Oh! Well caught!

CATTLEY: (*To KAY.*) I got that all wrong, didn't I? D'you know what this news is?

KAY: Do you fancy Mrs Morrison?

CATTLEY: Oh – she's tactile but untouchable, upper classy but very vulnerable, and some of us can't resist that, like smoked salmon lying on silver salvers. Go and fetch her. I've promised you a holiday in Normandy.

KAY: You're a coward, aren't you.

CATTLEY: No.

(*She goes to the field.*)

CATTLEY: I'm not a coward. (*To the audience.*) You can tell by my attitude to his racism. For some reason, the British middle classes like Israelis but not Jews. Distance lends enchantment, I suppose. As for the thrashing, well, really, (*Light laugh.*) he's not a fool. If he did that and was discovered, everything would disappear. (*Light laugh.*) And wasn't it Roger Ascham, tutor to Elizabeth the First, who said, 'Love is fitter than fear, gentleness better than beating, to bring up a child rightly in learning'? Well, love is all the rage just now, and the Head likes to be fashionable, so – (*Looking to the field.*) Nevertheless – Oh Martin, you look like Chekhov.

(*MARTIN has come in from the field and is looking for something.*)

MARTIN: I've lost my letter to Bobbie Thomas. It's on Basildon Bond, Blue, without an envelope to make it easier to flush away. It could ruin my career.

CATTLEY: Was it explosive?

(*They are both looking for it.*)

MARTIN: Enormously.

CATTLEY: Oh –

MARTIN: And will you tell Henry Hamilton next summer not to put me down for practice in the nets? I don't know what to do with leg breaks and googlies – I mean – the terminology –

CATTLEY: (*Still looking.*) Yes.

MARTIN: But actually, the real trouble is seeing them in white flannels. And I so love Latin.

CATTLEY: It's like falling off a bicycle, Martin. You have to get on again quickly, or you'll be terrified for life. You simply have to force yourself to face the white flannels.

MARTIN: You don't know what it's like, living among forbidden fruit, like Jerry Morrison. And they're so nice, all of them, so very nice.

CATTLEY: Morrison?

MARTIN: Don't worry, really, don't worry. I always manage.

CATTLEY: The obsessions that drive us all to do our jobs can be destructive.

MARTIN: What's your obsession?

CATTLEY: Don't be impertinent.

MARTIN: I was only –

CATTLEY: I've no intention of telling you.

MARTIN: Jerry Morrison is safe, John, I promise you. I really do. Smile?

CATTLEY: All right.

MARTIN: He's keen on Henry, anyway.

CATTLEY: He's what?

MARTIN: Sports. Cricket. Rugger. Very healthy. He's a clean living boy. Really. I know.

(*Enter KAY from the field.*)

KAY: Mrs Morrison says –

CATTLEY: Thanks for your reassurance, Martin. We'll talk later.

MARTIN: Oh. (*He goes.*)

KAY: Mrs Morrison says –

CATTLEY: The silly fool's lost three sheets of fantasy addressed to Bobby Thomas, Basildon Bond, Blue. Find it or there may be no holiday in Normandy.

KAY: That's what you want.

CATTLEY: No, it's not. Where's Mrs Morrison?

KAY: Waiting to talk to her son over tea.

CATTLEY: I'll go and prise her away. (*He leaves.*)

KAY: (*Calling after him.*) She's his mother! (*To audience.*)
Sometimes I seethe. I seethe!
(*Enter JANICE from the building.*)

JANICE: Ah. Free for smokers.

KAY: I'm going to leave them all.

JANICE: (*Smiling.*) Dear Kay, they all depend on you.

KAY: That's just a fantasy.

JANICE: I know.

KAY: Don't be smug. (*She exits to the building.*
JANICE sits and lights a cigarette.)

JANICE: (*To the audience.*) I teach Art here. No-one likes that,
but the results are stunning, so I'm worth a good deal to
the accountants. The mothers are keen on self-expression
because they think it's civilising. That's because they don't
see most of it. There's a lot of pain about.
(*Enter MONTY from the building.*)

MONTY: Are you saying things you shouldn't?

JANICE: I'm the only one who doesn't.

MONTY: No-one stops me talking. (*As he lights cigarette, to
audience.*) It's often peaceful here. I'm married and live out.

JANICE: (*To audience.*) I live out, too, some of the time.
(*Off clapping, a bit more than before. They both smoke
peacefully and smile at each other. Enter ADELAIDE.*)

ADELAIDE: They've stopped for tea. (*She sits.*) I'm sick of
women recommending gites in the Dordogne when I'm
about to stay with my sister in Prestatyn.

MONTY: Car insurance always comes up when you least
expect it, doesn't it?

ADELAIDE: Haven't you a diary?

MONTY: Mrs Monty has, but she never looks in it.

ADELAIDE: That's the sort of excuse I simply cannot tolerate.

MONTY: Mrs Monty takes Mogadon.

ADELAIDE: You all think too much. Just teach and play
cricket.

JANICE: That's death.

ADELAIDE: There must be more to life than death.

MONTY: I wonder what it is.

(*Enter CATTLEY.*)

CATTLEY: (*Of cigarettes.*) Put those out. Mrs Morrison's coming when she's finished her tea.

MONTY: She likes cigarette smoke, and she's going to break out one day.

JANICE: Not her.

(*Enter HENRY.*)

HENRY: Come on, we're fielding next.

MONTY: Give us time.

CATTLEY: (*Cigarette butt.*) Pick that up.

HENRY: The boys are getting their pads on and the others are ready. You're at wicket, Monty so –

MONTY: Don't aggravate me.

HENRY: I was only – oh, for goodness sake, Martin, we're fielding.

(*MARTIN has appeared eating a bun and looking for his letter.*)

MARTIN: I've lost something.

MONTY: And Mrs Morrison is coming up to see us.

MARTIN: What?

HENRY: I'll miss Jerry on the rugger tour.

JANICE: You will?

CATTLEY: I'll miss him for Henry the Fifth.

JANICE: (*Laughing.*) Oh no!

CATTLEY: We haven't had it since the Falklands.

MONTY: That was a different world.

HENRY: I was still at school.

MARTIN: I was a student and against it, brave me.

HENRY: It was thrilling.

JANICE: You were ten. Is it still thrilling?

HENRY: I haven't thought about it.

MONTY: (*Anticipating some fun.*) Adelaide thinks about it. She was a teacher in Hackney, and has particular memories, don't you, Adelaide?

MARTIN: Oh, not this.

(*JANICE chuckles and remains seated throughout all that follows.*)

CATTLEY: She went into the classroom – thirty-two of the famous underprivileged –

MONTY: And they were playing Exocet Missiles.

ADELAIDE: And I was the Argentine airforce. Sit down Robert.
(*MONTY, playing a boy, buzzes close to her ear.*)
Angela, you've taken off your blouse and bra.

CATTLEY: (*Playing a young girl with breasts.*) Twin missile launchers, Miss.

ADELAIDE: And what are you doing, Ahmed?

MONTY: (*As Ahmed.*) Ah'm Randy Andy in his helicopter, Miss, and this is mah joystick.

CATTLEY: (*In time with MONTY, both chanting.*) Joystick, joystick, joystick. (*Etc.*)

ADELAIDE: Put your joystick away, Ahmed, before –
And put Bella down, Lee.
(*As Lee, CATTLEY has begun to pick up MARTIN, helped by MONTY.*)

CATTLEY: She's a torpedo, Miss.

MARTIN: I always have to be the torpedo.

ADELAIDE: (*To MONTY.*) Just put her down, Denzil, before she explodes.

MONTY: (*As Denzil.*) She's going to explode, Miss –

CATTLEY: (*As Lee.*) Because she's in the exclusion zone.

MONTY: And she's headed for the Belgrano.

CATTLEY: And the Belgrano, Miss –

BOTH: Is YOU!
(*They charge at her using MARTIN as a battering ram and with the top of his head hit her in the stomach.*)

ADELAIDE: Stop it! Ah! (*She falls.*
MARTIN has his head in her lap.)

MARTIN: (*Scrambling to his feet.*) Oh – really.

MONTY: Bella landed with her head below the waterline, and punched till Adelaide was winded.
(*CATTLEY and MONTY have been laughing but it dies down.*)

ADELAIDE: (*Getting to her feet.*) It was very demeaning in Hackney. It is very demeaning to be winded.

HENRY: (*Turning away.*) Oh God. Oh tree!

CATTLEY: Don't fret, Henry. You're quite safe.
(*He begins to recite solemnly and alone at first, but joined eventually by everyone except JANICE. He has his arm round HENRY. Quite soon he conducts the whole group singling out some lines for solos and some for group reiteration.*)
This day is called the feast of Crispian;
He that outlives this day, and comes safe home,
Will stand a tip-toe when this day is named,
And rouse him to the name of Crispian.
He that shall live this day, and see old age,
Will yearly on the vigil feast his neighbours,
And say 'Tomorrow is the feast of Crispian.'
Then will he strip his sleeve and show his scars,
And say 'These wounds I had on Crispin's day.'
Old men forget; yet all shall be forgot,
But he'll remember with advantages
What feats we did that day; then shall our names,
Familiar in his mouth as household words,
Harry the King, Bedford and Exeter,
Warwick and Talbot, Salisbury and Gloucester,
Be in their flowing cups freshly remember'd.
This story shall the good man teach his son;
And Crispin Crispian shall ne'er go round
From this day to the ending of the world,
But we in it shall be remembered;
We few, we happy few, we band of brothers.
(*Silence. They are all in some kind of pose, perhaps with their arms round each other.*)
CATTLEY: (*Smug.*) And the Berlin wall came down, you see.
(*A brief silence. JANICE snorts. They all look at her. From the field enters MRS MORRISON.*)
MRS MORRISON: Goodness, have I interrupted something?
CATTLEY: Ah! We were rehearsing for the end of term concert.
MRS MORRISON: It's nice to see you're human.
CATTLEY: Yes. Well, the match, gentlemen – once more unto the breach.
MONTY: Mrs Morrison.
ADELAIDE: Mrs Morrison. (*They both leave.*)

MRS MORRISON: I found this. (*It is the letter.*)

CATTLEY: Oh.

MARTIN: Oh.

HENRY: Oh.

MRS MORRISON: I didn't read it.

CATTLEY: Ah.

MARTIN: Ah.

HENRY: Ah.

(*She hands it to HENRY who is nearest.*)

HENRY: Thank you. We're going to miss Jerry in the scrum.

MARTIN: That's mine.

CATTLEY: This is Henry Hamilton, games and junior –

MRS MORRISON: (*Smiling.*) Hello!

HENRY: You can see where Jerry gets it from.

MRS MORRISON: Gets what?

HENRY: Everything – haha!

(*MRS MORRISON laughs.*)

JANICE: Oh Henry, you are a joke.

MRS MORRISON: Pardon?

JANICE: Nothing.

MARTIN: (*To HENRY.*) The letter.

HENRY: Goodbye. (*To MARTIN.*) She gave it to me.

JANICE: Your son's art is very good.

MRS MORRISON: Thank you. He says good things about you, too.

JANICE: Yes. (*She leaves for indoors as the two men tussle over the letter as they to leave for the field.*)

MARTIN: Give it me!

HENRY: Ow!

CATTLEY: That was Janice. Art.

MRS MORRISON: (*Of the two men now out of sight.*) Are they all right?

CATTLEY: I'm sure they are. We'll all miss Jerry, Mr Morrison. (*She sits.*)

MRS MORRISON: Is that what you've asked me up here to say?

CATTLEY: Actually, no.

MRS MORRISON: It's the sweet shop again. (*She laughs.*)

CATTLEY: He keeps breaking the school rules.

MRS MORRISON: Mm. (*Then a little laugh.*)

CATTLEY: Learning the rules is what rulers have to do.

MRS MORRISON: Mm.

CATTLEY: Mm?

MRS MORRISON: Well, you're right. As I've told you, I did look at the state schools, and, well – against my true feelings about things – you know, about, well, things – I sent Jerry here because those places were running wild. I mean they were. Running wild. I didn't want him to be brought up in chaos.

CATTLEY: No. Though as I remember it, Jerry's home is very beautiful.

MRS MORRISON: His home? Oh yes, ours. I love it.

CATTLEY: You did most of it yourself, so it has a special, personal –

MRS MORRISON: What are you getting at, Mr Cattley?

CATTLEY: Jerry is not being brought up in chaos, but in beauty.
(*Silence.*)
We both love lovely things, you, your home, I, my work here.

MRS MORRISON: Mm.

CATTLEY: One might say we shared a kind of spirituality, an understanding of what lies behind beautiful things, and also what lies behind things that are not perhaps so obviously –
(*MARTIN has appeared looking sheepish and stands half trying to catch CATTLEY's attention.*)

CATTLEY: (*Seeing him.*) Martin? Aren't you fielding?

MARTIN: Long stop. Sorry. I wanted a word.

CATTLEY: I'm having a word.

MARTIN: About, you know?

CATTLEY: No.

MARTIN: Oh. Sorry. I was worried for a moment.
(*He goes.*)

MRS MORRISON: Is he all right?

CATTLEY: Yes. I do love my work here, Mrs Morrison. It's my life.

MRS MORRISON: What's Jerry really done?

CATTLEY: The sweet shop again –

MRS MORRISON: Does it matter?

CATTLEY: I think he's anxious to move on, doesn't feel he fits in. We all feel that way at times, the end of term –

MRS MORRISON: Mm.

CATTLEY: Mm?

MRS MORRISON: Well you know. Finding things out. It's quite big.

CATTLEY: You too? Well – finding things out for Jerry might mean his coming home to your beautiful house a few days earlier than he normally would.

MRS MORRISON: What?

CATTLEY: Is that a problem?

MRS MORRISON: Well – I love having him at home – of course, of course I do – but he'll miss the end of term and get bored like children do with their parents. I mean we are boring.

CATTLEY: It might also just go on his report to Winchester that his individualist behaviour –

MRS MORRISON: It can't. He's passed his common entrance, got his place, we've paid you for it.

CATTLEY: Yours is a truly nice family, Mrs Morrison. I'm sure nothing serious need be said.

MRS MORRISON: Are you?

CATTLEY: The fact is, we think – it isn't certain – we think – the head thinks – Jerry's managed to get hold of some nasty substance. Cannabis, in fact.

MRS MORRISON: You let him do that?

CATTLEY: Us?

MRS MORRISON: Well, I didn't. He's in your charge for nine months of the year.

CATTLEY: And together – together – we can see he doesn't go any further with this.

MRS MORRISON: He's a lovely boy. You're lucky to have him in your school.

CATTLEY: Very lucky, extremely lucky, he'd've been wonderful in Henry the Fifth. And the Head does see a solution to this really rather minor problem. You remember the brochure that brought us together?

MRS MORRISON: Individual care, fostering the natural talents –

CATTLEY: Yes. Yes. And I believe you signed a disclaimer form to say that if it became necessary to give your son a few – (*Laughs.*) – gentle pats with a slipper you would not withhold your consent.

MRS MORRISON: Did I?

CATTLEY: Mm. And this is the moment when the Head feels it might –

MRS MORRISON: No. There's a law against that now.

CATTLEY: I'm glad you feel that way.

MRS MORRISON: Why did you raise it?

CATTLEY: The Head looks at it like this. Jerry has tip-toed towards the drug culture. If we were to send him back to a lovely home, and to a lovely mother, that is a loving mother, it might not act as a complete deterrent. But if he gets, say, three or four whacks with a slipper, or actually, the threat of three or four whacks with a slipper, because, as you say – anyway, if that happened so that he went back afterwards to you, to your gentle care, and your beautiful home, that might be the saving of his future.

MRS MORRISON: I hear what you say.

CATTLEY: As it is, Jerry will simply be asked to leave early.

MRS MORRISON: Expelled?

CATTLEY: That's certainly not a word I intend to use, and nor if I have anything to do with it will anyone else. Look, obviously a woman of your quality needs – must need – time to think about the value of any kind of punishment for Jerry. Like me, you are a true liberal.

MRS MORRISON: How d'you know?

CATTLEY: Your house, your clothes, your conversation, the way you move – and of course, your decision to enrich Jerry's mind here. Does your husband share your views? On – everything?

MRS MORRISON: Yes, of course. What does liberal mean?

CATTLEY: Selecting the best above all things, and using common sense to see it feeds both the individual and the community.

MRS MORRISON: What's common sense?.

CATTLEY: Well – doing what is possible, and not following a dream.

MRS MORRISON: Is there a difference between a dream and a vision?

CATTLEY: We all need to have one of those, of course.

MRS MORRISON: What's your vision?

CATTLEY: Now?

MRS MORRISON: Mm.

CATTLEY: Gracefulness. In thought, movement, expression, surroundings –

MRS MORRISON: You're flattering me.

CATTLEY: (*Who is.*) I'm answering your question.

MRS MORRISON: Are you truly a spiritual man, Mr Cattley?

CATTLEY: Yes.

MRS MORRISON: I'll have to think about Jerry. We had such fun over tea. I'll leave him playing cricket, and I'll ring you up or something.

CATTLEY: I have to be down your way about six. I could call and help clear your mind.

MRS MORRISON: My husband's – We could discuss the pyramid outside the Louvre as well as Jerry. My husband's away.
(*MARTIN appears again.*)
I thought you were being long stop.

MARTIN: I thought you'd finished.

MRS MORRISON: We have. (*She leaves, passing him.*)

CATTLEY: What now?

MARTIN: That sod Henry has got my letter, and he might do awful things with it.

CATTLEY: Then get it off him. Go on. Between overs.
(*MARTIN goes.*
To the audience.) My obsession – my obsession is that I can't bear to be excluded. (*He leaves.*)
(*The light changes to early evening. Empty stage. Sound off of boys leaving. Bell. Silence. Grace muttered. Sound of boys leaving. Enter HENRY, limping slightly and with a bruised eye. He carries a small table that has glasses and a decanter of port on it. He is no longer dressed for cricket but wears a blazer and grey flannels. He pours himself a glass of port and takes a mobile phone from his pocket and dials a number.*)

HENRY: Trish? I'm ringing from the staff lawn. Oh, we won.
Yes, it was – okay. Look, can you really only have two
weeks off this summer? Well, do you have to have a job?
Yes, I know about careers, I have one too. It's just I'm
terribly lonely.
(*MORRISON has entered in his normal clothes: a school
uniform.*)
Yes, Morrison?

MORRISON: I want to talk to you, sir.

HENRY: I'm busy.

MORRISON: Please?

HENRY: (*To phone.*) Hello? I've got to go. It's a boy. Don't
make that sort of joke, Trish, it's dangerous. I'll ring later.
(*Phone away.*) Now Morrison, what seems to be –
(*MORRISON falls to his knees and putting his head in
HENRY's lap, bursts into tears.*) Oh Jesus. (*The tears continue.*)
Are you sure I'm the person you want?
(*The tears are slowly drying up.*)

MORRISON: I want to be safe.

HENRY: You're that with me, certainly.

MORRISON: I don't mind being punished. I don't want to
leave here.

HENRY: Punished? What for?

MORRISON: It's not the punishment that matters.

HENRY: What is it, then?

MORRISON: I just don't want to go away

HENRY: I do understand how you feel, Jerry. It's a big world
out there. We have to be brave.

MORRISON: It's not so much big as boring.

HENRY: Big and boring. That's why we have to be brave,
because being bored is a terrible thing. Why are you going
to be –

MORRISON: Can I ask my mother if you can stay in the
holidays?

HENRY: Oh gosh – Why me, all of a sudden?

MORRISON: I like you.

HENRY: It'd be lovely, of course. Your mother's very special
and –
(*Enter MARTIN, also in his normal clothes.*)

MARTIN: Oh!

HENRY: What?

MARTIN: I see.

HENRY: What do you see?

MARTIN: A hypocrite. I'll black the other eye if you like.

MORRISON: Did you do that, sir?

MARTIN: Yes indeed.

MORRISON: That was horrible.

HENRY: It's all right, Morrison.

MORRISON: It's not, it's dreadful. He's jealous.

MARTIN: I'm not

HENRY: What of?

MARTIN: Nothing. Unless of course –

HENRY: No!

MORRISON: What?

HENRY: You'd better leave us.

MARTIN: Yes.

MORRISON: No.

HENRY: We'll talk again.

MORRISON: You all say that.

HENRY: Who does?

MORRISON: Everyone. (*Moves off. To MARTIN.*) Swine.
 (*Gone.*)

MARTIN: He's been to the village again, you know.

HENRY: What did you think was happening here?

MARTIN: Love.

HENRY: Well, it wasn't.
 (*Mobile phone rings.*)
 Affection was happening here. (*To phone.*) Yes? It was
 nothing, Trish. I said nothing. I'll ring later. I said later.
 (*Puts phone away.*) Why did he say you were jealous?
 (*MARTIN is getting port.*)

MARTIN: Because I want affection.

HENRY: We all want affection. And they're so nice.
 (*Silence.*)

MARTIN: (*To audience.*) We're drinking port because we won
 the match. We drink it every night, as a matter of fact;
 sherry before dinner and port afterwards. It impresses us.
 (*To HENRY.*) I want affection very badly.

HENRY: Well, so do I. And I've a nasty feeling several cricket bats are missing from the pavilion.

MARTIN: You're changing the subject.

HENRY: No, I'm not. I love cricket bats.

(*Enter ADELAIDE.*)

ADELAIDE: Why is Morrison crying? (*She gets port.*)

MARTIN: Henry was fondling him.

HENRY: I was not fondling him. He was unhappy about something and doesn't want the term to end.

ADELAIDE: That's no reason to fondle him.

(*Enter MONTY in day clothes.*)

MONTY: Why is Morrison crying? (*Gets some port.*)

ADELAIDE: Henry was fondling him.

HENRY: He was unhappy and he cried.

MARTIN: On your lap.

HENRY: It wasn't my idea.

ADELAIDE: He wouldn't cry for me.

MONTY: I never tried to make him cry for me.

MARTIN: Can I have my letter?

HENRY: No.

MONTY: What letter?

HENRY: A filthy letter he wrote to Bobby Thomas about –

MONTY: For goodness sake, we've got more to worry about than that.

MARTIN: What, for example?

MONTY: I don't know. Exam results.

MARTIN: They're all right, aren't they?

ADELAIDE: Of course.

MONTY: Then what about your rugger tour to France?

ADELAIDE: You've got a black eye.

HENRY: It's nothing. Yes, the rugger tour, the cricket bats –

MONTY: What cricket bats?

HENRY: I think some people are collecting them as souvenirs.

MARTIN: Did you do that at school?

(*Enter JANICE.*)

JANICE: Why is Morrison crying?

HENRY: He's going to be punished.

JANICE: That's not why he's crying, so he says.

MONTY: You can't believe what people say.

MARTIN: What d'you mean, you can't believe what people –
MONTY: People always say they don't mind things, here. It's on the curriculum.
MARTIN: I mind things. You're drunk.
MONTY: I'm not.
ADELAIDE: He's always like this after the staff match.
MARTIN: Well, I mind him being aggressive, and I mind not having Bobby Thomas to look at, and I mind that hypocrite fondling Jerry Morrison, and I mind that bitch having what she calls Life Classes.
JANICE: The Head has had a word.
MARTIN: For or against.
JANICE: For.
ADELAIDE: Are they completely – ?
HENRY: Nude?
JANICE: There's a word for you, Henry.
MARTIN: It's disgusting.
HENRY: (*Producing letter.*) It's not as bad as 'Darling Bobby'.
MARTIN: Give me that!
HENRY: I won't!
MONTY: Why not?
HENRY: Because I want him to stop doing it! I want my paradise back, clean and proper and lovely!
MONTY: Are you going to blackmail him ?
HENRY: If I have to.
JANICE: Who's blacked your –
MARTIN: You – (*Lunges at HENRY.*)
HENRY: Stop.
MONTY: Stop!
ADELAIDE: Oh !!
  (*JANICE is amused. MONTY goes to intervene.*)
MONTY: For goodness sake. Stop behaving like a pair of children!
  (*In the struggle, a glass gets pushed into MONTY's face. He howls and staggers away from the other two who look horrified. He clutches at his face. Enter KAY.*)
KAY: Why is Morrison – oh good heavens!
MARTIN: I'm sorry, Monty, I'm dreadfully sorry.
HENRY: (*Still with the letter.*) I think it was me.

MARTIN: It was me.

HENRY: It was me!

MARTIN: Me!

MONTY: (*Blood running down his face.*) I'm bleeding to death!
(*Some sobs from all the men.*)

ADELAIDE: Be quiet! The Head'll be out here soon, and
you're all behaving like – like he said.

KAY: Come along Monty, I'll fix you up, there's a good boy.
(*A bell off.*)

MONTY: Who's taking prep?

KAY: One of the others. (*She leads him off, sobbing quietly.*)

MARTIN: It wouldn't have happened if you'd given me –

HENRY: Or if you'd never written it.

JANICE: Or if you really were the people you pretend to be.

ADELAIDE: No-one is the person they pretend to be, Janice.
That's why we're creative.

HENRY: I don't pretend. I'm completely myself, which is
why I play games.

MARTIN: And I'm completely myself, which is awful.

JANICE: But it's all so simple. Just be authentic. Be centred.
Feel the pain, love your innermost cool places, stay quiet.
(*There is a silence.*)

HENRY: (*Very quietly.*) Oh tree.

MARTIN: Tree?

JANICE: That's why I teach the boys simple, naked beauty,
and have them draw things that would scare their parents.
Then they'll have something to remember here that isn't
false. I'm going to bed now. Goodnight (*She leaves.*)

MARTIN: Should we rehearse Linden Lea?

ADELAIDE: Why does one love art so much more than artists?

HENRY: She's very popular with the mothers.
(*Enter the HEADMASTER. He is carrying a cane.*)

HEADMASTER: Ah. The select few. The other staff rarely
use this lawn, I notice, so it's become very special to me,
and I thought I'd have a discreet word – two discreet
words – with you, the few, before the term ends. First, it
now appears, from a phone call I've just received, that a
member – a distant but distinct member – of the House of
Windsor is considering coming here next term.

HENRY: Good Lord!

ADELAIDE: At last!

MARTIN: But what about Rupert, the trades unionist's son?

HEADMASTER: It'll do him good to rub along with the
monarchy. There's been no announcement in the press,
or indeed anywhere, in case of terrorism, of course, and
fear that the local yob culture might decide to take envious
action if the news got out. I trust, therefore, that you three
won't say anything to anyone at all, especially the visiting
staff, musicians and so on, until I give the word. Yes?
(*General assent.*)
The second, less pleasant but very necessary word, is that I
intend publicly to humiliate young Morrison tomorrow for
his behaviour over the village shop. I believe, and this is
very confidential, that he's been dabbling in drugs.

ADELAIDE: Drugs?

MARTIN: Drugs?

HENRY: Drugs?

ADELAIDE: Does Matron know?

HEADMASTER: I've no idea, but she's discreet to the point
of dumbness, so –

HENRY: It can't be true.

ADELAIDE: Corporal punishment has been banned, even
among the privileged.

MARTIN: He's pure as driven snow.

HEADMASTER: We must assume so, since he's one of us.
As for corporal punishment, if it became necessary I
should expect complete loyalty from my staff as well as
the student body.

ADELAIDE: It's illegal, Headmaster.

HEADMASTER: Yes. Yes. Yes. Yes. It is, however, necessary to make an example, even though the little liar denies
everything.

ADELAIDE: But surely the House of Windsor wouldn't send
a child to a school where corporal punishment –

HEADMASTER: Good heavens Adelaide, the House of
Windsor has been in need of corporal punishment for a
very long time.

(Enter CATTLEY from the field entrance, looking very full and satisfied.)

Ah, John, the very man.

(CATTLEY proceeds to the port table, in a long movement.)

CATTLEY: *(To the audience.)* I'm not going to tell you a thing but it was marvellous.

HEADMASTER: John?

CATTLEY: The answer is no. Use some other form of humiliation if you must do it at all. *(He pours out his own port.)*

ADELAIDE: You look victorious.

HENRY: I'd like to have a word with you, actually, about cricket bats

MARTIN: And so would I, about Henry.

HEADMASTER: Please leave us will you.

HENRY: But –

MARTIN: This is vital.

ADELAIDE: You're looking wild eyed, Herbert.

HEADMASTER: Out.

CATTLEY: You're holding a cane.

HEADMASTER: Out!

HENRY: *(As they leave CATTLEY and the HEADMASTER.)* It can't be true, Martin, about the drugs.

MARTIN: I can't believe it, not of Jerry.

ADELAIDE: He looks thoroughly disturbed, John. Herbert, that thing is absolutely –

HEADMASTER: I am not at all disturbed. Nothing disturbs me about intervening to make the young successful. *(He whacks the cane. Whack. Whack.)*

ADELAIDE: *(Leaving.)* You'll be prosecuted.

HEADMASTER: Only if someone sneaks, and we don't teach that here. *(To CATTLEY.)* So?

CATTLEY: I promised it would be something else, since that's been forbidden so as to bring us into line with the state system. *(Indicates cane.)*

HEADMASTER: Our parents don't pay twelve thousand pounds a year to be in line with the state system. They pay it to escape from the state system – no, John, don't interrupt. And a good thrashing never did me any harm. *(Whack whack whack.)*

CATTLEY: You would be breaking the law.

HEADMASTER: We make the law.

CATTLEY: We certainly lead but we don't –

HEADMASTER: Yes we do, everyone knows we do, and that's why they come here.

CATTLEY: I said you wouldn't.

HEADMASTER: There's nothing in the brochure about not doing it.

CATTLEY: I gave my word.

HEADMASTER: Where? (*Silence. HEADMASTER sniggers.*) Aha aha aha. A very private promise, I think? A secret promise, never to be divulged? No wonder he's not head boy. Like mother, like son. I hate Jerry Morrison. He's devious, he's manipulative, and he's manipulating me, going in all innocence to the village shop as if he were a clean-limbed lad simply bending trivial rules and showing golden individuality when all the time he was trafficking in God knows what.

CATTLEY: Manipulation is what we teach, Herbert. The boys can't confront us, so they play games with us. That's what people recognise when they see the word initiative in the brochure – breaking the rules and not getting caught. Surely you should be very proud of Jerry Morrison because he passed the test so well.

HEADMASTER: He's trying to outmanipulate me, and that's unforgivable. He's forcing me to behave illegally to show the world – or parts of it, anyway – that we are morally serious people who will not tolerate drugs. Now here's a word, John. Our brochure will soon contain the crested phrase – By Appointment To The Royal Family. (*Whack whack.*) What about that, eh?

CATTLEY: You mean –

HEADMASTER: I can't tell you who, but yes.

CATTLEY: Oh Herbert, well done! And the bank will be pleased.

HEADMASTER: It will, it will, and not before time, though education's beginning to go our way again, with the discovery of Middle England. So somehow I must make a fearful example of Jerry Morrison, much too clever by half,

171

or it will all go wrong (*Whack.*) Oh, we know what we're doing, you and I. You sound off about the arts and the need for individual attention, but it's breeding we sell here. Mrs Morrison may want her son to learn computers and history and stuff in all gentleness, I've no idea, but she sure as hell wants him to have a smattering of good tunes and long words, to stand up straight and play squash, and keep his hands in his pockets while talking to the tradesmen.

CATTLEY: She's not like that.

HEADMASTER: She may not want to be, but she's joined the club. She wants a nicely spoken boy who can tell other people what to do. Of course he does strange things in the art class but, basically, Mrs Morrison sent her boy here to learn moral rectitude. Or the appearance of moral rectitude, that is, breeding. And this (*The cane.*) – or something else if I can think of it – will teach him how to do it, and keep the covenants rolling in from the old boys to finish the new wing for girls, and don't you go making postcoital promises I don't intend to keep. (*Whacking rhythmically through the next sentence.*) Because we're going to get a Royal next year. What is it now?

CATTLEY: I haven't said anything.

HEADMASTER: Your silence is venomous.

CATTLEY: You're doing wrong.

HEADMASTER: What?

CATTLEY: Wrong.

HEADMASTER: Wrong?

CATTLEY: Wrong. I wish I hadn't said that.

HEADMASTER: It's not a word we use here, except to children. Morrison's done wrong; our word is difficult, a word with ambiguities, your sort of word. And if I have to I shall do this last difficult thing to put him right. Difficult decisions are always the ones that hurt other people, you know, to make them better, and often they are above the unimaginative law. (*He prays, holding up his cane, eyes shut.*) Help the strength of my arm, oh Lord, with the strength of Thine. (*Whack.*) Out there are drugs, violence, values in flux, income tax –

CATTLEY: There is no hint of Mozart in this, no French
poetry, no Henry the Fifth –

HEADMASTER: Oh, good old Catfish, almost radical
Catfish, always one for the apt reference, exactly what
you're here for, but I can tell you this, my friend – there's
only one phrase that counts in all the hundreds of
quotations spouted at me about education over the years,
all the lace tracery of poetry and painting and philosophy,
Jung, Freud and all those – Israeli thinkers – there are only
three pungent words I've ever heard that mean a brass
farthing. 'Does – it – work?' So tomorrow I'm going to
humiliate that smart-arsed, brassy-faced, defenceless boy in
a chilly ceremony to stop his bad reputation losing us our
income, our salaries, our Royal Family, and all that goes
with it in our lovely land, John Cattley, and it will work.
We shall all still be here, staff, parents, children, Royals,
art, all sticking together because we know our way is best.
And you are going to stick around while I do it, as you
have done before, and you will moan a bit, and then you
will go on working here because you like living among
nice people who think you're nice too, and Morrison's
humiliation isn't going to stand in your way for a minute.
Well, maybe for a minute, while you're angry with me and
sorry for him, and then you'll find the right quotation and
all will be well inside your twitching stomach. You will
stand by Jerry Morrison as he staunches his little tears,
and you will put your arms around him and you will say,
unbelievably, but rightly, 'Jerry,' you will say, 'Jerry, it was
a case of being cruel only to be kind.'

CATTLEY: If you use that, I have to say you'd be putting me
in a very difficult position.

HEADMASTER: Oh no. Loyalty is simple.

CATTLEY: (*Quiet fury.*) Give it me.

HEADMASTER: No.

CATTLEY: Give it me!

(*They wrestle for the cane. HERBERT in fury whacks him
across the cheek. He puts his hand up and takes it away
with some blood on it. There is a scar.*)

(*Very upright, in great pain, and through gritted teeth.*) I shall, of course, ignore that, Headmaster.

HEADMASTER: (*Very primly indeed.*) I should think so. And don't let's have any more frivolous behaviour, Mr Cattley. You're a responsible adult in a responsible institution. I've had a word about it, and I shall now spend the night in my study contemplating the difference between genuine compassion and liberal expediency. Who knows what I shall decide?

(*ENTER MONTY and KAY, MONTY with a large bloodstained bandage round his eye and head.*)

Goodness, Monty. Got something in your eye?

MONTY: A glass.

HEADMASTER: That'll teach you not to keep rough company. (*He leaves.*)

KAY: John, you're bleeding.

CATTLEY: I promised her he wouldn't break the law.

I've been quite brave, actually.

KAY: Did you sleep with her?

CATTLEY: What's that to you?

MONTY: (*Lighting a cigarette.*) I hate the end of term.

KAY: I love you.

CATTLEY: Oh – what's love?

KAY: Don't be so pernickety. (*She pulls at him.*)

CATTLEY: What are you doing?

KAY: I'm going to give you things people in large conversions haven't thought of yet.

CATTLEY: I taught you most of them.

KAY: And what's more, I'm angry. Seething! (*She pulls at him to get his offstage.*)

CATTLEY: What has happened to your eye?

MONTY: I think I may have lost it, but we aren't saying anything in case we accidentally spill the beans about Martin and –

KAY: Come, John.

(*She pulls him towards the house.*)

CATTLEY: You aren't supposed to smoke on the staff lawn.

(*They are off, and MONTY smokes and sips port.*)

MONTY: (*To audience.*) I shouldn't even be here, since I live out, but this might scare Mrs Monty. (*His eye.*) It's her night for the cinema with friends and I wouldn't want to spoil that.
(*Bell off.*)
Bed time for the juniors. They're so nice, and it's not their fault they're here.

End of Act One.

ACT TWO

Night on the staff lawn. The table and the port and the glasses are still there. There is moonlight. A light goes on inside the building entrance and stays on. MORRISON and JANICE enter in pyjamas and dressing gowns. MORRISON is carrying a blank canvas. They pause for a second on the lawn.

JANICE: Not here. (*They go off towards the playing field.*
Enter CATTLEY in his dressing gown only. There is a large piece of sticking plaster on his cheek. He follows a little way and then turns to address the audience.)

CATTLEY: (*To audience.*) That's why Herbert never made him head boy. I hope she doesn't go doing risky things like that with the Royal Family – whatever risky things they are. I suppose I could go and look, but somehow just now – someone might ask what I was doing, wandering about at this time, dressed in – and his mother knows a thing or two about me which – And anyway he leaves tomorrow – today – after he's been – whatever the Head – I don't want to know any more! I only came out here to clear my brain, which is spinning, oh spinning, and I'm so tired!
(*Enter KAY in a dressing gown.*)

KAY: Are you being a schoolmaster or a human being?

CATTLEY: What does it matter? (*Laughs a little helplessly.*) I'm searching for balance.

KAY: Balance is simply a way of saying that you're right and everyone else is wrong.

CATTLEY: I don't know what's got into you. You're like the sea, all of a sudden, with little flashes of phosphorus illuminating the dark for a tiny second and then all those long, dragging loins and heavy shadows.

KAY: I heard you tell the headmaster what I do and I realised what it is. It's madness. I do madness, and it's good.

CATTLEY: It's not.

KAY: Oh yes.

CATTLEY: Just at this moment there is a stone vulture sitting up there, ready to drop on me, over and over, in heavy,

176

brainsplitting cracks, demanding that I offer up my account of what I've done. (*To KAY.*) Stay there. It nearly kills me every time it falls on me, and lays me out, and measures me, waiting for me to struggle to my feet. (*To KAY.*) Don't move! And as I lie there, I feel as if my life – isn't. Hasn't. Won't. Doesn't – quite. It's as if I'm – just – just. I don't know who you – where you – is this – I mean – where?

KAY: Here, on the staff lawn. Come to me, and stop gesturing at the sky in that European way. (*She pulls him down beside her.*)

CATTLEY: You're not saying useful things, Kay.

KAY: I'm doing sweet things, John.
(*CATTLEY kneels up, having been got into the position of being astride her.*)

CATTLEY: I'm Catfish.

KAY: Your name's John.

CATTLEY: John doesn't know how to answer. He's up there, somewhere, arguing with vultures.

KAY: (*Hugging his body.*) Concentrate on this body which I adore. (*Roving hands.*)

CATTLEY: Not a lot of use without me in it. (*Trying to wriggle free.*) Aoh!

KAY: (*Trying to hold him.*) You're there, all right. I can hear you.

CATTLEY: It's just my voice. John Cattley? Come in, John Cattley. I want you back. It's a question, really, of whether I join him out there or he joins me in here.

KAY: Is this all because of Mrs Morrison and her perfumed soul blossoming in the conversion?

CATTLEY: It's because her son visited the village shop on the wrong day. Stop it.
(*Enter MONTY, dishevelled looking, the bandage still round his eye and head.*)

MONTY: Still busy with the end of term arrangements? I just wanted a glass of port to take away the pain. Damn.
(*He spills a little as he pours. To audience.*) I've been sleeping in the common room. Are you all right, John?
(*CATTLEY slowly rises to his feet, authoritatively.*)

CATTLEY: Have you ever known me when I wasn't?

MONTY: I've never known you in that position. Are you all right, Kay?

KAY: (*Still on floor.*) Interrupted, but all right.

MONTY: Is it preparation for when we take girls?

KAY: We were being primitive.

MONTY: Mrs Monty will have taken her Mogadon by now. I hope you don't expect me and Adelaide to –
(*ADELAIDE enters in night dress and dressing gown with her book and a tooth mug.*)

ADELAIDE: Are you dead, Kay?

KAY: D'you want a list of the exam results, or next year's form order, or –

ADELAIDE: No, thank you.

MONTY: What brought you out, then?

ADELAIDE: (*Pouring a large port.*) The smell of doom. That poor boy, lying in his bed, waiting for – does the head know what he's doing?

CATTLEY: Herbert says he's simply going to humiliate the boy, expel him, exclude him –
(*Enter HENRY in pyjamas and dressing gown.*)

HENRY: Hello!

MONTY: I suppose once he's gone I can see a doctor without the fear of revealing awkward things – (*In pain.*) Oh!
(*He starts to roll a joint.*)

HENRY: (*Getting port.*) I've found a prep school near Arles that makes the rugger tour absolutely perfect.

CATTLEY: Oh good.

HENRY: I thought you'd be pleased. I couldn't sleep for excitement.

ADELAIDE: (*Seeing the plaster on CATTLEY's face.*) Good heavens, John. Did Kay do that to you?

CATTLEY: No, the Headmaster. I really think we ought to go in to try to get some sleep, don't you?

ADELAIDE: If we could.

MONTY: Which we can't.

ADELAIDE: Was it some form of assessment?

HENRY: (*Now with a glass of port.*) I've only just got here.

CATTLEY: It's not a midnight feast, Henry. What are you doing, Monty?

MONTY: Oh –

HENRY: Are you all right, Kay?

CATTLEY: Monty?

MONTY: It's just a roll-up.

KAY: (*Still recumbent.*) How's your nice Patricia?

HENRY: Nice? I love her.

KAY: Madly?

HENRY: Well –

KAY: I see. (*Getting up.*) Would you like some port, Mr Cattley?

CATTLEY: Well –

MONTY: That's very formal, considering how –

KAY: I feel like a vulture.

CATTLEY: No!

HENRY: I do love her madly (*To ADELAIDE.*) – and what do you put in that book?

ADELAIDE: It's my time table and lesson planner.

HENRY: You still plan your lessons?

CATTLEY: It's merciless of you to raise the vulture.

KAY: (*Pouring port for him and herself.*) I'm not here to be merciful.

CATTLEY: Then be polite. The world must be polite.

KAY: That's a lot, Adelaide. (*She hands CATTLEY his port. MONTY lights up.*)

(*Enter MARTIN in pyjamas and dressing gown.*)

MARTIN: Have you deliberately left me out?

CATTLEY: Of course not. Go to bed.

ADELAIDE: (*Taking more port.*) It's like ribena, really. Is that cannabis?

MONTY: Yes.

HENRY: Monty!

CATTLEY: You said it was just a roll up.

MONTY: It deadens the pain. And anyway, you know I smoke.

CATTLEY: I order you to put it out.

MONTY: It's the end of term.

CATTLEY: I don't care what it is –

MONTY: Oh shut up.

CATTLEY: But the head – Morrison –

ADELAIDE: What got you up?

MARTIN: I'm worried about the letter, I'm worried about me, and I'm worried about his mobile telephone.

CATTLEY: Mobile – do you have one?

HENRY: To organise rugger tours and speak to Trish.

CATTLEY: What about?

HENRY: Private things.

CATTLEY: Assignment making?

HENRY: Yes.

KAY: (*Laughing.*) He fancies Janice.

HENRY: Don't be silly.

KAY: She doesn't fancy you.

HENRY: I know she doesn't.

MARTIN: It's Morrison, actually.

CATTLEY: What?

HENRY: It isn't.

MARTIN: Oh, we know.

CATTLEY: What do we know?

HENRY: Nothing. Jerry's lonely, that's all.

CATTLEY: Jerry? What is all this?

HENRY: Nothing, nothing, nothing.

ADELAIDE: Perhaps his phone is just for comforting chat.

HENRY: It is.

CATTLEY: Right. That's harmless, just what we need, so put
  that out and everyone go to –

HENRY: Can't we just enjoy being out here in the moonlight?

KAY: Aah, isn't he sweet.

MARTIN: (*With a glass of port.*) Not really. He reads my letters
  to the editors of the tabloid press.

CATTLEY: You can't.

HENRY: I don't.

CATTLEY: You're sure you don't?

HENRY: Of course.

MONTY: Trish's father would pull the stories anyway.
  He wants so much to join the establishment, he wouldn't
  let us down.

CATTLEY: I only ask because – I might as well tell you – and
  keep it to yourselves – and then pull yourselves together,
  and stop (*Indicates joint.*) – we're going to have a member of
  the Royal Family here next term.

HENRY: Yes.

ADELAIDE: Yes.

MARTIN: Yes.

MONTY: What?

KAY: It's been fixed, then?

CATTLEY: You know?

ADELAIDE: The Head said we three were reliable.
(*Slight stagger.*) The others are to be kept ignorant,
especially the visiting musicians.

MONTY: Well, I'm reliable. I have been for years,

CATTLEY: He didn't tell me he'd told – you knew it might
happen?

KAY: He swore me to secrecy.

CATTLEY: But you're only the school sec – the absolute,
thoroughgoing, double-crossing sod! I'm Catfish, the
highly cultivated Deputy Head of Chantrey's, the finest
prep school in the south of England!
(*There is a shocked silence.*)

MARTIN: (*To HENRY.*) Well!

CATTLEY: (*To KAY.*) And you knew?

KAY: There were more important things –

CATTLEY: We're all losing our perspectives, telling people,
not telling people, having words in the wrong ears –

KAY: No we're not.

CATTLEY: We are. And him smoking that stuff and the head
threatening to break the law.

ADELAIDE: It smells lovely.

CATTLEY: And what's this about Morrison and Henry?

HENRY: I'm not like that.

CATTLEY: I know. That's why we appointed you.

MARTIN: Who did you ask?

CATTLEY: It was obvious.

MARTIN: Not to everyone.

HENRY: What d'you mean?

MONTY: The Head's going to cane that boy in the morning,
I'm sure of it. He's ridiculous.

CATTLEY: I'm the only one who can say that sort of thing,
me, Deputy Head. And he's not going to cane the boy, I've
given my word about it, and anyway he can't. It's just that
he has to do something. For all our sakes he has to show this
school to be a morally serious place where Royalty can –

ADELAIDE: (*Looking to the playing fields.*) There's someone out there.

CATTLEY: What? Oh – rabbits. It's rabbits. I've told the groundsman.

MARTIN: If you've said things about my letter on that phone, I'll say I saw Jerry Morrison on your –

HENRY: I've said nothing! I love this place!

CATTLEY: On your what?

KAY: D'you want me to go and see what's happening out there? (*Taking the joint from MONTY.*) Thanks.

ADELAIDE: Yes.

CATTLEY: No. It's much safer for all of us to go to bed. Alone. (*Of joint.*) And give that back.

KAY: Who d'you think it is, then?

CATTLEY: No-one. But if it is someone, they might be vandals or the press or someone else we shouldn't meet in dressing gowns and bandages, smoking illegal – stop grinning, Monty.

MONTY: It's nice.

MARTIN: What's happened to your cheek?

KAY: The Head hit him.

MARTIN: Having a word?

ADELAIDE: He's wrong to cane that boy.

CATTLEY: He's only going to humiliate him, Adelaide.

ADELAIDE: It's illegal and wrong.

CATTLEY: Whatever he's doing, he's doing it for us! (*Calmer.*) He may be a sod, but he's doing it for us, rooting out something rotten so the rest of the flowers can bloom. And he believes it's right. (*To ADELAIDE.*) Leave the port alone.

ADELAIDE: (*To MONTY.*) Can I try that?

CATTLEY: Adelaide!

ADELAIDE: (*To CATTLEY.*) Do you want it?

CATTLEY: I'm a man of letters.

(*KAY hands it over to ADELAIDE.*)

CATTLEY: Adelaide, come on. Think of Hackney.

HENRY: I understand about rooting things out.

MARTIN: You're dangerous, Henry.

HENRY: I'm ordinary.

MARTIN: (*Smiling.*) You're not.

HENRY: I am.

ADELAIDE: Jerry Morrison is lovely, and it's wrong to humiliate him, even if we do all believe in family values.

CATTLEY: The Head feels very strongly for young Morrison, and he wants –

MONTY: Who believes in family values? This is a boarding school.

ADELAIDE: I believe in family values.

MONTY: You haven't got a family, that's why.

ADELAIDE: I've got a sister.

MONTY: Prestatyn doesn't count.

ADELAIDE: Ooh! No wonder Jerry Morrison likes this.

HENRY: This place is my family. To me it's home.

MARTIN: To me it's home.

KAY: And the boys are so nice. Is anyone else prepared to confess?

CATTLEY: It's our work, where we do the thing we do, and that is all, and unless we –

ADELAIDE: Where do you live, then John?

CATTLEY: In my mind. The world of beauty and ideas, France –

HENRY: Good food.

MARTIN: Wine.

MONTY: A lot of that.

ADELAIDE: Cannabis.

CATTLEY: I don't need cannabis.

MONTY: Anyway, that's Holland.

HENRY: Can I try it?

CATTLEY: Henry!

(*ADELAIDE hands joint to HENRY.*)

KAY: He lives with vultures, haunted by the past.

CATTLEY: Oh traitor! You and the Headmaster, treacherous as bats. Those vultures are mine and no-one else's.

MARTIN: (*To HENRY, who is puffing away.*) Give me that letter.

HENRY: No.

MARTIN: Please.

HENRY: No!

(*There follows a struggle, HENRY still with the joint in his mouth.*)

CATTLEY: What are you doing?

MARTIN: Saving things. Ow – ow! (*He is in considerable pain. He has sprained his wrist.*)

HENRY: Oh God.

MARTIN: It's only a sprain.

HENRY: I'm sure it's more than that. Kay?
(*She takes the joint.*)

MARTIN: It's not, it's not. Please. Don't. Oh, thank you.
(*HENRY takes off a square or scarf he is wearing and is making a sling for MARTIN and fitting it. The others have made small ineffectual movements to help but actually stand looking on. Then ADELAIDE, moving to get more port:*)

ADELAIDE: How touching to see one man caring for another.

MONTY: One young man caring for another young man. 'Thy need is greater than mine.' Sydney.

CATTLEY: Sydney who? Oh, Sir Philip, yes, very classical. Now, let's all go to bed and sleep.

ADELAIDE: Sleep that knits up the ravell'd sleeve of care –

CATTLEY: Shut up.

KAY: Poor Catfish.

CATTLEY: It must be clear, even to you, that if we're photographed by the gutter press out here getting smashed in our pyjamas at 2 a.m. the palace might find it surprising.

KAY: So you think that (*The previous noise by the field.*) is the press, closing in on us in our finest hour –

HENRY: Well, I haven't said a word to anyone. I wouldn't. Thanks. (*KAY hands the joint back to HENRY.*)

MARTIN: You really wouldn't?

HENRY: I truly wouldn't.

MARTIN: Really?

HENRY: Truly.

MARTIN: You're surprisingly kind.

HENRY: Well – (*Adjusting the sling.*) – a friend in need is a friend indeed.

MARTIN: Good heavens. Thank you.
(*HENRY has handed him the joint and they both smile.*)

MONTY: Can I have it back soon? I paid for it.

MARTIN: Just a minute. (*Puffs.*)

CATTLEY: Oh – Please!

ADELAIDE: Herbert is asleep in his study and I'm going to go to him and I'm going to wake him up, and I'm going to say that it is wrong to flog that little boy. Who's coming?

CATTLEY: We've been into it all, Adelaide, I've told you, and he understands the position very clearly. Everything is for the best – Mozart, Shakespeare, Kipling, Robert Bridges –

ADELAIDE: 'Time, you old gypsy man, will you not stay, Put up your caravan, just for one –'

CATTLEY: That isn't Bridges.

MONTY: (*Taking back the joint.*) Thanks.

KAY: She's right, Catfish.

CATTLEY: She's not. It's a minor poet called William Brighty Rands, who –

KAY: You know she's right, we know she's right, everyone outside will know she's right. You can't be sure how Herbert's going to jump. Let's go and wake him up, and tell him it is absolutely clear that he must not cane – or even humiliate – Jerry Morrison.

CATTLEY: He's the headmaster.

KAY: Oh for God's sake, John, this is only a prep school! (*Silence.*)

CATTLEY: I don't think you should say things like that, with the new golf course and sports complex and computer centre and girls coming and the Royals and classes in the state sector going up again, and the league tables – We're the answer to society's needs in the twenty-first century. For heaven's sake – I don't know how we can bring everything back into proper perspective if you say things like 'It's only –' We are guardians of the best young minds – their parents have chosen us to be –

(*MARTIN kisses HENRY lightly on the cheek. HENRY bridles and then they both kiss on the lips. HENRY eventually withdraws from the kiss.*)

CATTLEY: Henry?

HENRY: I didn't mean to do that.

MARTIN: I didn't mean to do that – exactly.

HENRY: And I didn't like it.

MARTIN: I didn't either, quite.

HENRY: In fact, I hated it.

MARTIN: You didn't hate it. You were trying it out, I could tell.

HENRY: I was trying it out, and I decided to hate it.

MARTIN: If you decided to hate it, you didn't actually hate it, because you can't decide how you feel about things, you simply feel them.

MONTY: They kissed each other, John.

CATTLEY: I know, and I can't think of anything to say to them.

ADELAIDE: You could say, 'How was it for you?' Isn't that the phrase people use in matters of bodily experience?

KAY: How was it for you, Catfish?

CATTLEY: Tiring. I'm just so tired, and my cheek hurts.

MONTY: (*Offering joint.*) Here.

CATTLEY: No.

> (*HENRY's mobile phone rings out. He takes it from his dressing gown pocket. Everyone stares at it.*)

HENRY: I didn't realise it was turned on.

CATTLEY: Do answer it.

> (*He does.*)

HENRY: Hullo? Oh, it's you. (*Giggles.*) Yes, I'm fine. Yes, I know I said I'd ring you back. We're on the staff lawn. No, it's not a party; we're having a kind of discussion. What about? Well –

> (*Varying interest in the reply. CATTLEY alarmed.*)

Nothing very important.

> (*MARTIN touches him, places a hand over his or some similar gesture of complicity.*
> *HENRY makes a little flinching noise.*)

Nothing's wrong. No, it isn't, really it isn't. Nothing's bloody well wrong! All right. I'll tell you next week, when we meet. (*Phone off. To MARTIN.*) Stop that.

MARTIN: Will you tell her about me?

CATTLEY: Please not.

HENRY: I've told you what that was. And they say a man should try everything once.

MONTY: (*Getting more port for himself and ADELAIDE.*)
Sir Thomas Beecham said that a man should try everything once except incest and Morris dancing.

HENRY: It's just I feel lonely. I feel lonely, he feels lonely, we all feel lonely. It's a Latin verb, isn't it, Martin.

CATTLEY: Don't turn witty. I order you all for the last time to go to bed.

ADELAIDE: Oh no. Let's practise Linden Lea for the end of term concert, and then go and defeat Herbert, and make sandwiches in the kitchen to celebrate.

CATTLEY: All right, then. Linden Lea. Get into line.

KAY: What are you doing?

CATTLEY: I'm doing what I can to get things back.

KAY: They won't go back.

CATTLEY: They must. This is about values, Kay, world leadership and art. The world needs us, because we're right. It's impossible that we are wrong so the Head won't cane Jerry Morrison, because he can't, so come on, Linden Lea, and then bed.

(*The others are stumbling into line.*)

MONTY: We need a music teacher.

ADELAIDE: They're all peripatetic.

MONTY: Well tried.

HENRY: There's trouble with cricket bats.

CATTLEY: Ready?

HENRY: They keep them as souvenirs.

CATTLEY: One, two, three.

(*CATTLEY starts conducting them in Linden Lea. KAY comes forward to him as he does so on her knees and begins to fumble with his dressing gown. He attempts to push her away. The others, facing the entry into the house, begin to stop singing as they see the HEADMASTER arriving.*)

ADELAIDE: Herbert?

(*CATTLEY whips round to see the HEADMASTER, and adjusts his dress as he does so.*)

It is wrong to cane Jerry Morrison, and we're against it even if he is in love with Henry.

MARTIN: Or Henry's in love with him.

HENRY: (*A squeak.*) No.

CATTLEY: Adelaide, I've told you that, whatever happens, it is the Head's decision.

HEADMASTER: Upon the King! Let us our lives, our souls
　　Our debts, our careful wives,
　　Our children and our sins lay on the king!
　　We must bear all! What infinite heart's ease
　　Must kings neglect, that private men enjoy!
　　And what have kings, that privates have not too,
　　Save ceremony, save idol ceremony?
　　And what art thou, thou idol ceremony?
　　What are thy rents? What are thy comings in?
KAY: Twelve thousand smackers a year per pupil. I'm the
　　secretary. I get the cheques.
HEADMASTER: Why is everyone wearing bandages?
MARTIN: Henry kissed me, Headmaster.
HEADMASTER: I'm sure he had his reasons, but don't do it
　　again, there's a good lad. Latin masters are hard to come
　　by.
KAY: John Cattley and I have been doing all sorts of –
HEADMASTER: I noticed, and I wish to know and to say
　　nothing more. (*Sniffs.*) The atmosphere smells funny.
MONTY: It's the horse chestnut.
　　(*There are giggles off.*)
　　What's that?
CATTLEY: Nothing.
KAY: Mr Cattley says it's rabbits.
HENRY: Rabbits. Pardon.
　　(*The mobile phone goes.*)
　　Oh!
　　(*HENRY takes it out of his pocket.*)
HEADMASTER: Yours? Well, answer it.
HENRY: It's only Trish.
ADELAIDE: Only?
HENRY: Not only. It is.
HEADMASTER: Answer it.
HENRY: I don't want to.
HEADMASTER: I'm having a word, Henry. Speak to your
　　girl friend, and tell her everything is fine.
　　(*HENRY answers the phone.*)
HENRY: Hullo? Yes, I'm still – No, I've told you, it's not a
　　party.

MARTIN: (*Towards the phone.*) It is a party and he kissed me.

HEADMASTER: Sh!

HENRY: I didn't.

CATTLEY: (*Calling towards the phone.*) It's insignificant! Patricia, it doesn't matter!

MARTIN: It does to me.

CATTLEY: Patricia, my dear, he loves you!

HENRY: How d'you know?

HEADMASTER: Your future depends on it.

MONTY: (*Calling.*) Someone shoved a glass in my face.

CATTLEY: That's insignificant, too!

HENRY: Nothing's going on. I'll talk to you in the morning. There. (*He ends the phone call.*)

MONTY: It matters a hell of a lot that my eye is bloody well hurting, Catfish.

HEADMASTER: If there's trouble with Trish's father, just remember that we've got new buildings, the National curriculum, parent governors, only one retired colonel on the board, girls coming to live in, we've abandoned the concept of thrashing for the concept of humiliation, and above all, the House of Windsor –

CATTLEY: I told you, I told you, he's abandoned it.
(*Enter JANICE and MORRISON with the canvas. They cross the stage. All are surprised into silence. As they are leaving:*)

CATTLEY: What've you been doing, Morrison?

HEADMASTER: I'll deal with this, Mr Cattley. What've you been doing, Morrison?

HENRY: Stealing cricket bats, that's what he's been doing.

MORRISON: Don't send me home early, sir. Don't send me away.

JANICE: It'll be alright, Jerry.

HEADMASTER: Jerry?

MORRISON: Don't send me home.

CATTLEY: We probably won't.

HEADMASTER: We certainly will.

JANICE: Go on now, love. I'll see it's all right.

MORRISON: Promise?

JANICE: Promise.

MORRISON: And you promise, Mr Hamilton.

HENRY: Yes. What?

MARTIN: I love you, Jerry Morrison.

MORRISON: Oh, you love everyone, sir. (*He goes into the house.*)

HEADMASTER: What was all that about? (*To MARTIN.*)
Especially that?

HENRY: I think he meant it as a compliment.

HEADMASTER: And what's all this about promising? (*Sniffs.*)
Do you smell funny?

JANICE: That boy has a soul and you are damaging it.

MARTIN: I don't love everyone. Love is particular.

CATTLEY: The headmaster is well aware –

JANICE: And you know quite well, Cattley, that you are
teaching this boy a rigid attitude of submission to hierarchi-
cal authority that –

CATTLEY: What are you doing?

JANICE: I'm empowering him.

HEADMASTER: I'm empowering him, giving him the authority that goes with received pronunciation. You do smell
funny, everything smells funny.

JANICE: Jerry Morrison needs self-realisation, personal
awareness, love, and somebody to hug.

HEADMASTER: I knew it! You've been touching him. Head
boy indeed. Let me tell you, that we have a golf course, a
sports complex, a computer centre, separate wash basins in
the dormitories –

JANICE: And no-one to touch him in case the press finds out.

HEADMASTER: Of course not, especially as we're going to
take in girls, let alone others.

CATTLEY: Have you traumatised him, Janice?

JANICE: You've traumatised him.

KAY: The culture vulture.

CATTLEY: Quiet.

HEADMASTER: Just go to bed, all of you, to your own personal beds, without cigarettes.

HENRY: I hate this evening.

MARTIN: No you don't.

ADELAIDE: I want to touch Jerry Morrison. Now all the
youth of England is on fire –

CATTLEY: You can't touch him, Adelaide,

ADELAIDE: Everyone else does, why can't I?

HEADMASTER: I was not angry since I came to France till now! You're all obsessed with sex.

MONTY: Ah, now, sex. I know something about sex that no-one else does.

CATTLEY: You do?

HEADMASTER: Has Hammerstein been at you, as well?

MONTY: Sex is a matter of souls, Herbert.

HEADMASTER: Who said you could call me –

MONTY: Souls facing souls, naked except for their tingling skin. This is a fact, however, which has been distorted, and wrestled almost out of our minds by nothing else than bigoted, frightened, racially prejudiced Christianity.

HEADMASTER: Racially – you have been at him. (*To CATTLEY.*) Or you, with your priapic lack of discrimination.

MONTY: Why d'you think the dying Christ is always shown wearing a loin cloth? The Christians say it's because to see the funny bits of God would be sacrilegious. They don't complain about those hoary old flashers from Greece, though, do they, always flaunting their parts. Nor the naughty statuettes of Buddha and his girl friends, jig jig. No, the real reason Christ is always pictured in a loin cloth is that no Christian could bear to see that the tip of his John Thomas was snipped off, and that he was Yiddish and not a thoroughly respectable white Anglo-Saxon protestant goy. There.

HENRY: For goodness' sake.

MARTIN: Please!

HEADMASTER: Just because you're good at maths, there's no need to convert to Einstein's relig… (*Appalled.*) You're smoking one of those things.

MONTY: It's true, though. We've been taught to hide from lovely old sex because of anti-semitism.

CATTLEY: I hadn't thought of that. It could be true, Herbert.

HEADMASTER: I knew we'd hear from your liberal libido.

CATTLEY: It's obvious when you think about it. We've established chastity as something deeply rooted in the modest figure on the cross, his privates covered in a hanky, when actually it's just we don't want to be reminded that the Son of God was Jewish down to the very tip.

JANICE: Or lack of it.

HEADMASTER: I have to say that none of this is at all relevant to the end of term as we are currently having to face it.

CATTLEY: What you're saying, Monty, is that we've perverted our knowledge of our basic instincts and our beautiful skin because of racial prejudice.

MONTY: Yes, I think that's – yes.

KAY: I think I've learned to understand my basic instincts and my beautiful skin pretty well.

HEADMASTER: I knew it! It is you, driving my staff out of their skulls. I tell you all, Chantrey's School for Boys is the home of virtuous Anglican beauty, the appreciation of the finer things, a seat of civilisation, so go to bed, and Hammerstein, I'm not having you handling the cheques a moment longer. You're fired.

KAY: Thank you. I'll leave the account books, which you don't understand, beside the instruction book for the computer, and I'll put the photos of the parents on your desk so you'll learn to recognise them by yourself, and I expect you'll settle on a new source of bulk lavatory paper –

HEADMASTER: There are more important things in education.

KAY: As for Christ, if he'd been a woman, no-one would've dreamed of putting on a loin cloth. You'd all have wanted a jolly good look up her whenever you got on your knees of a Sunday morning.

CATTLEY: Well, the female form doesn't have the incriminating parts that –

KAY: Don't try to teach me things. Before I came along you thought a tongue was just a thing for making speeches with. I never knew a teacher yet who admitted to learning anything.

HEADMASTER: You're fired, three times over, fired, fired –

KAY: (*To MONTY, and taking the joint.*) Can I have that?

HEADMASTER: Put it down.

KAY: It's nothing to do with you, now. I'm free.

MARTIN: If you won't give me my letter, give me another kiss.

HENRY: Stop it.

MARTIN: It's all this talk of privates.

HENRY: Why don't you play rugger?

HEADMASTER: You're driving them mad, you see. You're what we used to call a witch.

JANICE: I think I'll go to bed.

HEADMASTER: Just one minute. I want to see that canvas.

JANICE: If you promise not to send Jerry home early.

HEADMASTER: Possibly.

(*JANICE displays a totally blank canvas.*)

HEADMASTER: There's nothing there.

JANICE: We didn't get around to painting.

HEADMASTER: I've been tricked. No painting, so Morrison goes home early – with great relief on my part. Ha!

JANICE: If he goes home, I'll tell his mother what we did out there.

CATTLEY: What did you do?

HEADMASTER: Nothing! We don't want to know.

MONTY: I do. What was it?

JANICE: Oh come on, Monty.

HEADMASTER: I'm going to bed, we're all going to bed, this is just a passing nightmare. Tomorrow I shall thrash Morrison –

ALL: No!

CATTLEY: Humiliate, you said humiliate!

HEADMASTER: – well – well –I'll certainly send him home, and we shall have the end of term concert in the evening – Linden Lea, among other things, without the tableau vivant. The boys, apart from Morrison, will sing Non Nobis Domine as usual, and they will mean it. (*He sweeps out.*)

CATTLEY: What were you doing?

JANICE: Empowering him.

ADELAIDE: (*Gazing at the painting.*) They call this minimalist, I think.

JANICE: You need know nothing more, unless the Headmaster does something foolish in the morning, in which case I suppose the social services might get involved. (*She leaves towards the house.*)

HENRY: The social services?

MARTIN: Don't drool. You aren't thirteen.

CATTLEY: I don't care what happens any more. Herbert should've told me about the Royals. Dear Monty.

MONTY: Dear John. (*Offers the joint.*)

CATTLEY: No, thank you.

KAY: You won't be going to Normandy, now, will you.

CATTLEY: I'll have to find a replacement.

KAY: Come along, Adelaide, the Almost Leader of the Almost Liberal Tendency.

ADELAIDE: (*As she is led out.*) Did we get anywhere about the thrashing?

KAY: Possibly, we don't know.

ADELAIDE: The boy will tell people.

KAY: They're all very loyal, Adelaide.

ADELAIDE: And so nice.

MONTY: (*To the audience.*) We'll still be here next term, you know. Try how they might, they don't ever quite get rid of us, because we know how to imitate what's best out there and make it expensive so people feel they have to have it. Even our new buildings look like a shopping mall, so everyone believes we're up to date, and they like the fact that we're eccentric with it. Does the youngsters a power of good, they say. (*To the others.*) See you at prayers for humiliation. (*He goes.*)

MARTIN: You're very unhappy.

HENRY: I want to speak to Trish.

CATTLEY: What are you going to say?

HENRY: That I love her.

MARTIN: Then I'll tell her that you didn't really kiss me.

HENRY: Will you?

MARTIN: Let's go in and be private.

HENRY: You're very kind.

MARTIN: You're very kind.

HENRY: No, it's you who's very kind.

MARTIN: It was you who started being kind. (*They are off.*)

CATTLEY: (*To audience.*) I am a lover of the beautiful; I cannot bear to be excluded; and I am suddenly alone. This is not how I planned my lovely life. I must decide certain moves,

choose which nettles must be grasped, even make state-
ments. And I don't know what they are.
(*Enter MRS MORRISON from the field, wearing jeans
and a waxed mac.*)
MRS MORRISON: I had to come
CATTLEY: Yes, I suppose –
MRS MORRISON: You overturned me.
CATTLEY: Could you refresh my memory?
MRS MORRISON: Your sense of beauty and grace, your
understanding of the poverty of riches –
CATTLEY: I love riches.
MRS MORRISON: But differently from me, the me who
was, before you. I had to talk to you about – well, eternity.
CATTLEY: I'm going to have to honour all that, aren't I.
MRS MORRISON: It did matter to you?
CATTLEY: Oh, it mattered. I just have other things on my
mind.
MRS MORRISON: I'm afraid I love you.
CATTLEY: No, you don't.
MRS MORRISON: Yes, I do.
CATTLEY: (*Pretty desperate.*) But I hate the pyramid outside
the Louvre.
MRS MORRISON: I know how I feel, Mr Cattley. You told
me things about the effect of beauty on the world, how
even the true appreciation of a French construction could
make society a better place, and you did it with your hands
covering my skin, quivering me, and your lips whispering
– You're a God.
CATTLEY: We've been talking about God this evening, actu-
ally. And skin.
MRS MORRISON: Please will you kiss me?
CATTLEY: (*Not doing so.*) There's been quite a lot of that here,
too.
MRS MORRISON: I want to feel that sense of soul and body
again, now. (*She hugs him and lays her head on his shoulder.*)
CATTLEY: It's just that my soul is getting rather overworked
– the end of term, you know –
MRS MORRISON: You've been so good to Jerry.
CATTLEY: Ah.

MRS MORRISON: You actually are all the things you talked about.

CATTLEY: What did I talk about, apart from French constructions?

MRS MORRISON: The power of the imagination to alter the world. You were so – present.

CATTLEY: Mm.

MRS MORRISON: Mm?

CATTLEY: I mean yes. I was. I am.

MRS MORRISON: We both are.

CATTLEY: Normandy is awfully provincial, don't you think? Rather like Prestatyn, with cream.

MRS MORRISON: I adore you, John Cattley.

CATTLEY: (*To audience.*) John Cattley, adored. Mm. (*To MRS MORRISON.*) Honour, then. Let's go to the pavilion.

MRS MORRISON: Yes.

CATTLEY: (*As they go.*) You do believe the things I say?

MRS MORRISON: Is that all right?

CATTLEY: Yes.

MRS MORRISON: Oh – your cheek.

CATTLEY: I can't begin to explain it.

MRS MORRISON: I parked my car by the pavilion. I didn't use the Volvo. I came in the little rag-top.

CATTLEY: The little rag-top. Think of skin, John Cattley.
(*They have now left by the field exit.*
A cry from HENRY from inside the building.)

HENRY: Don't! Not now!

MARTIN: I'm sorry.
(*They both enter.*)

HENRY: Can't you see? She just didn't believe us so her father's sending some one down tomorrow.

MARTIN: I'm sorry, I'm sorry, I'm sorry.

HENRY: He'll find out about Morrison, Janice, drugs, you, Bobby Thomas – and all you can do is try to hug me.

MARTIN: We'll come through somehow. The Royals are coming, and they always come through.

HENRY: There's something happening down there.

MARTIN: Perhaps it's Catfish and Kay.

HENRY: Perhaps it's more trouble with cricket bats.

MARTIN: Who wants cricket bats?

HENRY: The poor.

MARTIN: What would the poor want with cricket bats?

HENRY: Who knows what the poor want? Envious bastards – I mean, I'm sorry, but they are. They probably want to attack us. I'd better go and –

MARTIN: Henry, if the ship's going down why don't we escape together?

HENRY: I don't want the ship to go down. There's the rugger tour to France.

MARTIN: I thought, perhaps, a little antique shop in Salisbury.

HENRY: No! (*Then.*) What are you doing in the hols?

MARTIN: I thought I'd go to Italy. Via Amsterdam.

HENRY: I've got a car. There is someone in the pavilion.

MARTIN: It'll be the poor. Let's go in. (*He reaches out his hand. HENRY slowly takes it. MARTIN puts his arm around him as they start to go in.*)

HENRY: It was just like this when I was a new boy at Sevenoaks. Tomorrow will be awful. (*They are off.*)
(*Lights change to full morning light. From the building comes the sound of morning prayers, and the whole school mumbling the Lord's Prayer.*
MRS MORRISON comes in without her waxed mac and sits, waiting. We hear the HEADMASTER's voice.)

HEADMASTER: Jerry Morrison?

MORRISON: Sir.
(*There follows more mumbling. MRS MORRISON looks at the car keys in her hand, stretches happily, and smiles to herself. Suddenly the voice of the HEADMASTER raps out.*)

HEADMASTER: So bend over!
(*We then hear the whack of a cane, unmistakeably a cane. MRS MORRISON immediately reacts, going to the entry to the house.*)

MRS MORRISON: Stop! That's a cane! Stop it!

MORRISON: (*Off.*) Shut up, Mum.

HEADMASTER: (*Off.*) Quiet!

MRS MORRISON: Stop that! It's illegal!
(*She goes in and is immediately brought out again by CATTLEY holding her arm.*)

Everyone from now on is in day clothes and, where necessary, bandages.)

CATTLEY: You're early.

MRS MORRISON: You said that wouldn't happen.

CATTLEY: Unhappily, the headmaster felt –

MRS MORRISON: I insisted.

CATTLEY: When Jerry's on these premises the Headmaster is in loco –

MRS MORRISON: Did you know last night he was going to commit a crime?

CATTLEY: Nothing was certain.

MRS MORRISON: You lied! All that talk.

CATTLEY: I meant every word of it.

MRS MORRISON: But it didn't stop you letting this happen.

CATTLEY: Things are never simple

MRS MORRISON: Oh, they are. You simply wanted me as your bit on the side.

CATTLEY: No.

(*From now on the rest of the characters in the play appear individually or in pairs and watch the argument between MRS MORRISON and CATTLEY. The last to appear is the HEADMASTER. He discreetly carries the cane.*)

MRS MORRISON: Of course you did. I wanted great things for Jerry and all I got was abuse.

CATTLEY: You knew quite well what you were doing when you sent him here. You were getting rid of your responsibility. What's more, you paid thirty thousand pounds to get him thrashed, so you must think it's worth it.

MRS MORRISON: I didn't pay to have the law broken on him.

CATTLEY: Thrashing was the law when you sent him.

MRS MORRISON: We expected value for our money. My husband works hard for his cash, a real man, rags to riches in fast food.

CATTLEY: I do know, and I wonder why I bothered.

MRS MORRISON: Are you a snob as well?

CATTLEY: Only about pretensions. Pretences, perhaps.

MRS MORRISON: I never pretend.

CATTLEY: Oh! If you'd been as motherly as you say, you could've kept your son at home. But no, you were quite happy to hand him over to complete strangers, me and my – as it happens – excellent colleagues, who are very skilful, all of them.

MRS MORRISON: Jerry says you're all bent as crooked pennies, one way and another.

CATTLEY: Our private lives have nothing to do with him, nor with you, nor with anything that happens here. Obviously you think so, too, or you'd have taken him away. Now something happens you don't care about and you wail and howl and stamp your feet like a little nine-year-old and say you didn't mean it to happen like this.

MRS MORRISON: It's you who's behaving like a nine-year-old, caught out with your talk of excellence and beauty, and the qualities of leadership. You try to pretend you're a great prophet, when all you are is a lousy prep-school master, resorting to assault and battery when you can't solve a problem any other way. You're a complete baby.

CATTLEY: I'm not a complete baby.

KAY: An incomplete baby.

CATTLEY: Don't you join in. If you want your son to learn the culture of the four letter word, Mrs Morrison, you can take him away and put him in a state school, where they don't do Henry the Fifth, I'll bet, or sing Linden Lea and Non Nobis Domine – running wild, you said, they don't even teach Latin.

MRS MORRISON: He knows the culture of the four letter word, like all of us.

CATTLEY: Learnt it from his manly father?

MRS MORRISON: From me, from everyone, from Shakespeare, so shut your fucking mouth.

CATTLEY: Breeding will out.

MRS MORRISON: Not from you, you cringing coward in your ivory tower of a boys' school.

HENRY: It's not an ivory tower

CATTLEY: Quiet, Henry.

HENRY: But it's not.

MARTIN: It is.

MONTY: It is.

HENRY: It's not, we're taking girls.

MRS MORRISON: It's an ivory tower where you can all pretend to be grown up because everyone else is prepubescent, though the reek of testosterone flooding in new and fresh is pretty heady.

KAY: You're witty. I thought you were just beautiful and full of folk music.

MRS MORRISON: Are you the school secretary?

KAY: Or the other woman, depending how you look at it.

MRS MORRISON: (*To CATTLEY.*) You deceiving, omnivorous bastard!

CATTLEY: I'm a man of exceptional stamina.

MRS MORRISON: Well, Jerry's leaving here and going to a comprehensive school.

MORRISON: I don't want to. I want to go to Winchester, like everyone else.

HEADMASTER: (*At his suavist.*) Everyone else doesn't go to Winchester, that's the point of it. It's the point of privilege the world over, much to be treasured privilege from the lion in his pride, the philosopher in his academy, to God, indeed, in his heaven – everywhere that the fashionable flood gates of democracy haven't rusted with their vile tinctures of equality. Knowledge is for the strong, to use as they see fit, in our society today as in all others. The strong, after all, are powerful, and the powerful are usually rich, so let us forget this little unpleasantness – most especially the infringement of the laws about drugs, and their illicit purchase – and let the boy stay for the end of term events as he desires, and then he can proceed with an unblemished reputation into the school he so admires.

MRS MORRISON: He's not staying here to be savaged one moment longer.

HEADMASTER: He won't be. (*Snaps the cane and throws it away.*) The blood has been let, now.

MRS MORRISON: Come along, Jerry.

MORRISON: No. (*He runs into the house.*)

MRS MORRISON: Jerry!

JANICE: You aren't fit to be a mother.

MRS MORRISON: Oh you, the earth thing! We had this sort of trouble with the au pair. Jerry?

HENRY: The thing is, we'll all have to leave. Trish has told the press I kissed Martin.

ADELAIDE: (*With smiles of delight.*) Oh! I remember! Sweet!

HEADMASTER: People often kiss Martin. I've had a word with him about it, so there's no need to worry.

HENRY: But they've found out everything. We are exposed.

HEADMASTER: Having done what?

HENRY: Kissing, smoking hash.

MONTY: Giving head to Catfish on the lawn.

CATTLEY: Where d'you learn these words?

HENRY: Trish heard it all on my mobile phone, so she told one of her Daddy's editors. And now there's this caning.

MRS MORRISON: There certainly is.

HEADMASTER: Oh no. The apex of British education is not to be denied me like that. I have worked all my life to be the perfect teacher in the widest possible sense, having the very best people under my care to make the very best people for my country, with family values and a love of cricket, and now I'm reaching the top, new buildings, Royalty, a trades unionist's son called Rupert, doing well in the league tables, even the hope of a documentary by the BBC, I'm not going to slide down to the bottom because someone has been careless with their mobile phone. I call on you all to use that virtue for which the private schools are most noted. Loyalty. We must stand together and win.

MRS MORRISON: I want my son. (*Calling.*) Jerry?

ADELAIDE: Jerry!

MRS MORRISON: He's not yours.

JANICE: (*To MRS MORRISON.*) Nor yours.
    (*MORRISON appears. He holds a cricket bat.*)

MRS MORRISON: Now come with me. (*She grabs at him.*)

MORRISON: I'm staying.

MRS MORRISON: You're not.

MORRISON: I am. (*He swings the bat and hits her on the head. She falls.*) This is where I belong. (*He goes to join JANICE, the others rush to care for MRS MORRISON. Not the HEADMASTER.*)

JANICE: There.

KAY: For goodness' sake.

ADELAIDE: Loosen things.

MONTY: You know how her clothing works, John.

CATTLEY: It's her head he hit.

MRS MORRISON: (*As he approaches.*) Don't touch me.

HEADMASTER: Morrison.

(*All turn to listen.*)

That is a school cricket bat and it should not be in your possession. You have deliberately taken it from a cupboard in the pavilion which you unlocked with a key you must've stolen from Mr Hamilton. I don't know what we're going to do with you, Morrison. The moment your sense of social responsibility is tested, you surrender everything we've taught you. Also, Morrison, that is your mother.

MORRISON: Yes, sir

HEADMASTER: Well, pick her up and comfort her.

MORRISON: I want to stay with you.

MRS MORRISON: (*Getting up.*) I'm all right.

(*A sound of a car.*)

HENRY: Here they come.

MONTY: The outside world.

HEADMASTER: Loyalty, then. Let's see it. – Who'll hold the bridge with me?

MORRISON: We will!

HEADMASTER: Good boy. You've learned a lot today.

MORRISON: Come along, please, and stand by the Headmaster. (*The staff move.*) That's right. (*To off.*) Ready.

MRS MORRISON: You little prig. And you, you shits, you absolute shits –

HEADMASTER: Language, you see.

(*A piano starts to play the introduction to 'Non Nobis Domine'.*)

KAY: Thank God I don't have to stay.

MRS MORRISON: Nor me.

(*They go.*)

HEADMASTER: I think we can let you go, now Mr Cattley. Rather too much Freud about you, if you understand my fairly complex meaning.

CATTLEY: You're excluding me?

HEADMASTER: And Henry, ring up Trish's father and tell him the establishment is being threatened by his gutter press, and will he call them off. He wants his knighthood. (*A boys' treble choir begins to sing 'Non Nobis Domine', Kipling set by Warlock, off. The staff join in haphazardly as they stand in a group by the HEADMASTER. Not CATTLEY or KAY.*)

CATTLEY: (*Over the music.*) All right! I've prevaricated for you till I'm rotten, Herbert, and manipulated till I can't say an honest word. I'm going now, and don't care, but I must add this; we all began by coming down tubes to grow in other tubes in an act of passion, and that passion must inform everything we do. It has to! Kay! Mrs Morrison! (*He runs out after them.*
The choir goes on and the staff sing loudly.
HENRY dials his phone.)

HEADMASTER: Well done, everyone. Splendid. It only takes a word, you see. (*To audience, smiling.*) That's how it works, usually. (*To HENRY on the phone.*) Well done, Henry. (*Singing continues.*)

The End.

By the same author

Summer Again
9781840025170